candybabies

cute crochet for wee ones

candi jensen

candy babies

cute crochet for wee ones
candi jensen

Sixth&Spring Books
New York

Sixth&Spring Books
233 Spring Street
New York, NY 10013

Editorial Director
Trisha Malcolm

Art Director
Chi Ling Moy

Photography
Dan Howell

Graphic Designer
Christy Hale

Stylist
Mary Helt

Copy Editor
Pat Harste

Technical Editor
Carla Scott

Illustrations
Ryan Brunetti

Yarn Editor
Veronica Manno

Intern
Susan Hoover

Project Manager
Michelle Lo

Production Manager
David Joinnides

President and Publisher, Sixth&Spring Books
Art Joinnides

Chairmen
Jay H. Stein
John E. Lehmann

Library of Congress Cataloging-in-Publication Data
Jensen, Candi
  Candy babies : cute crochet for wee ones / Candi Jensen
    p. cm
  ISBN 1-931543-54-2
  1. Crocheting—Patterns. 2. Infants' clothing. I. Title

TT825.J4297 2004
746.43'40432—dc22

200367343

Manufactured in China

introduction

Babies are definitely a blessing, and having so many in my neighborhood has always been part of the joy of living here. The wonderful little toddlers who inspired me so much with my first book are now going off to nursery school and elementary school—it doesn't seem possible. Luckily a new crop of babies is due on the same streets very soon.

My two-year-old grandson Johnny is also growing up—and out of the clothes he used to look so cute in. It pains me to know that he no longer fits into something that was lovingly made for him, but I still try to squeeze him into sweaters that show way too much of his belly and probably cut off the circulation in his arms.

Then one day, I had an epiphany: I could just make more sweaters. The mere thought of creating fresh designs for Johnny and all the new babies on the block became the inspiration for this book.

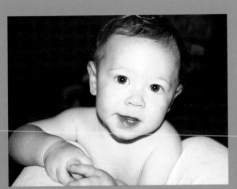

special garment that is much more fun. Just imagine a little tyke wearing a faux-suede jacket accented with shearling trim, or the "ugg" booties— who could resist?

I've also been inspired by today's yarns. Yarn has come a long way, especially for babies. You don't have to limit these projects to yarn you would normally think of as suitable for babies. Crocheting with novelty fibers in saturated hues will make a

As you look at the designs in this book, hopefully you'll find something to make for a special little one in your life. Though they'll undoubtedly grow out of it, you can always 'just make more'.

emerald isle
10/58

pastel parfait
12/60

in the navy
14/64

fine lines
16/66

east meets west
18/70

feet first
30/90

fur ever
32/92

poncho power
34/94

wrap star
36/96

warm front
38/98

baby bloomer
50/118

take a bow
52/120

hot step
54/126

c o n t e n t s

emerald isle

B old stripes in color-popping hues add plenty of verve to this quick-stitch sensation. A relaxed silhouette makes for an easy fit and the matching pants provide all-day comfort.

p a s t e l   p a r f a i t

This vintage-inspired hat-and-vest set is nothing short of fabulous for fashion-minded tots. Whimsical bobble accents and a faux-fur trim jazz up the tie-front vest while an oh-so-cute granny-square hat with earflaps completes the entire look.

i n t h e n a v y

Dynamic racer stripes and aqua-colored trim along the side seams offer plenty of spirit to this V-neck pullover. It's a cinch to stitch in half-double crochet and the relaxed fit takes this rough-and-tumble number day to night without missing a beat.

fine lines

A button-front romper rendered in a refreshing palette of berry hues takes Baby from playtime to naptime in style. Enhanced with a striking trim, this snazzy handmade treasure is a treat to make and, more importantly, a delight to wear.

e a s t   m e e t s   w e s t

Aluxurious trim and decorative frog closures take a sophisticated kimono sweater to new heights—it's the perfect attire for any formal occasion. And paired with the pretty dress on page 21, she'll be the belle of the ball!

orient express

Live the glamorous life in this darling dress fit for a princess. Drawing inspiration from the traditional Chinese cheongsam, this stunner features a single-crochet bodice trimmed in black and finished with a bountiful silk skirt. The complementary kimono sweater (page 19) makes an ideal cover-up.

blue dreams

When evening temperatures drop, this denim-inspired jacket is en vogue for the wee set. Mock pockets and stitch embroidery liven up a relaxed bodice, and the faux-fur collar and hemline make it extra-special.

v e s t   f r i e n d

What separates this chic button-front
vest from its store-bought denim
counterpart is the fact that Baby's version
will be handmade with love. It offers
more than just warmth: details such as
a running embroidery stitch, miniature
pockets, and fabulous faux-fur trim along
collar and hems make it superbly stylish.

living color

Paired with a simple turtleneck and pair of jeans, this multi-striped poncho offers a fuss-free fashion fix that's sure to please the most fashionable tykes. It's a perfect project to make with your leftover yarn stash, and works up in a flash in double crochet stitch. Hippy chic never looked this good!

g o l d e n   c h i l d

*C*hase away the chills with a gorgeous
shearling-inspired jacket accented
with a cozy faux-fur collar and cuffs and a
whimsical tassel on the zipper. Top it with
the dapper helmut hat with earflaps, and
you'll transform an outfit from ordinary to
extraordinary.

f e e t   f i r s t

Who needs to sacrifice style for comfort? At the heel of fashion, these up-to-the-minute fashion booties were inspired by traditional Australian sheepskin boots called "uggs." These one-of-a-kind booties are easy to hand-crochet in single and half-double crochet stitch; a faux-fur trim lends an authentic touch.

f u r   e v e r

A plush faux-fur coat caters only to those who want to live on the cutting edge of style! Dimensional novelty yarn lends maximum texture and single crochet stitch will have you whipping it up in a flash.

poncho power

Traditional Peruvian art inspired the
intricate design of this spirited
poncho. Work the easy silhouette in one
piece, create the design using half-double
crochet stitch and finish it off with fringes.

Alternate rows of single and crossed double crochet stitches create the lovely pattern on this sweet surplice top. The dainty picot edging adds just the right touch.

w a r m   f r o n t

When the termperature drops, keep your little one feeling toasty in this snazzy pullover and pant set. Worked in a luxurious wool/cashmere blend, the pullover has running trellises of cables across the front and single crochet edging, while the pants offer an elastic waistband for all-day comfort.

s u m m e r   l o v e

This beauty is a wearable for all occasions—from a stroll along the promenade to a picnic in the park. Subtle lacework, picot edging along hemlines and a pretty white ribbon lend rustic appeal to this short-sleeved dress.

a h o y ,   m a t e y !

From sea to shore, this nautical pullover with matching shorts will keep your cabin boy at the helm of fashion. The crewneck pullover features vibrant stripes across the body and matching buttons along left shoulder; elastic-waist pants keep this look casual.

t a n k   g i r l

This all-American set makes for a memorable first salute to Independence Day. Celebrate the occasion in high spirits with a striped tank top and matching pants that would make Uncle Sam proud.

party princess

She'll be oh-so-pretty in pink wearing this pint-sized cardigan over a romper or dress. This unique tie-front stunner is crocheted in one piece and features blanket-stitched accents along edges.

victorian charm

Ruffled lace and dainty pearl buttons over a dusty lavender bodice lend an antiquated touch to this vintage-inspired cardigan—it makes a treasured heirloom that can be passed on from generation to generation.

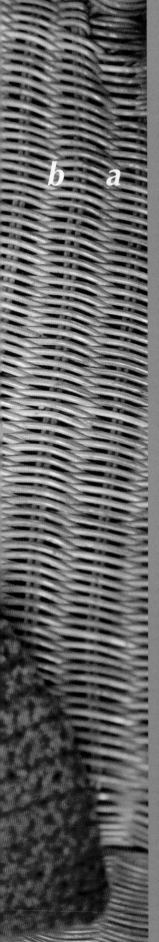

baby bloomer

A cuddly-soft romper adorned with a pretty floral appliqué will have her looking fabulous throughout the year. Crocheted in a single crochet stitch, it makes an ideal weekend project.

t a k e   a   b o w

Accent a basic cardigan with a cute gingham bow, and your small fry will be dressed to impress on the playground. Half-double crochet makes it a breeze to stitch and matching buttons complete the look.

h o t   s t e p

Feet first— stitch up your favorite
playtime pals on a pair of cutie
booties that are sure to draw smiles!
From bunnies to ducks, bears to dinosaurs,
these whimsical creatures—worked in
single and half-double crochet stitch—are
a blast to wear.

i n s t r u c t i o n s

SIZES

Instructions are written for size 6 months. Changes for sizes 12 months and 18 months are in parentheses.

FINISHED MEASUREMENTS

Pullover
• Chest 22 (24, 26)"/56 (61, 66)cm
• Length 11 (12, 13)"/28 (30.5, 33)cm
• Upper arm 9 (10, 11)"/23 (25.5, 28)cm

Pants
• Waist 21 (24, 26)"/53.5 (61, 66)cm
• Length 15 (16½, 18)"/38 (42, 45.5)cm

MATERIALS

Pullover
• 2 1¾oz/50g skeins (each approx 108yd/100m) of Tahki Yarns/ Tahki•Stacy Charles, Inc. Cotton Classic (cotton) in #3715 green (A) **4**
• 2 skeins in #3786 teal (B)

Pants
• 2 skeins each in #3715 green (A) and #3786 teal (B)
• Size G/6 (4mm) crochet hook or size to obtain gauge
• Two ¾"/19mm buttons
• ¼yd/.75m of ½"/13mm-wide elastic
• White sewing thread
• Sewing needle

GAUGE

15 sts and 20 rows to 4"/10cm over sc using size G/6 (4mm) hook.
Take time to check gauge.

NOTE

See page 130 for working color changes for rows.

STRIPE PATTERN I

Working in sc, work 4 rows A and 2 rows B. Rep these 6 rows for stripe pat I.

STRIPE PATTERN II

Working in sc, work 2 rows A and 2 rows B. Rep these 4 rows for stripe pat II.

PULLOVER

Back

With A, ch 43 (45, 49). **Row 1 (WS)** Sc in 2nd ch from hook and in each ch across— 42 (44, 48) sts. Ch 1, turn. Beg with 2nd A row, cont in stripe pat I and work even until piece measures 11 (12, 13)"/28 (30.5, 33)cm from beg. Fasten off.

FRONT

Work as for back until piece measures 9 (10, 11)"/23 (25.5, 28)cm from beg, end with a WS row.

Left neck shaping

Next row (RS) Work across first 18 (19, 20) sts, ch 1, turn. Dec 1 st from neck edge every row 3 (3, 2) times, then every other row twice—13 (14, 16) sts. Work even until piece measures same length as back. Fasten off.

Right neck shaping

Next row (RS) Sk 6 (6, 8) center sts, join color in progress with a sc in next st, work to end. Cont to work as for left neck, reversing shaping.

SLEEVES

With B, ch 23 (25, 27). **Row 1 (RS)** Sc in 2nd ch from hook and in each ch across— 22 (24, 26) sts. Beg with 2nd B row, cont in stripe pat I and inc 1 st each side every 4th row 6 (7, 8) times—34 (38, 42) sts. Work even until piece measures 7 (8, 9)"/17.5 (20.5, 23)cm from beg. Fasten off.

FINISHING

Sew right shoulder seam.

Neck edging/buttonhole band

From RS, join B with a sc in first st of left front shoulder, then sc in each st to within last st, work 2 sc in last st. Making sure that work lies flat, sc evenly around front neck edge, then cont along back neck and back left shoulder. Ch 1, turn. **Next row** Sc in each st across to left front shoulder, work 2 sc in corner, sc in next 1 (2, 2) sts, ch 2, sk next st, sc in next 4 (5, 6) sts, ch 2, sk next st, sc in each st to end. Fasten off. Sew on buttons. Fasten buttons into buttonholes, then pin left shoulder to secure overlap. Place markers 4½ (5, 5½)"/11.5 (12.5, 14)cm down from shoulders on front and back. Sew sleeves to armholes between markers. Sew side and sleeve seams.

PANTS

Left Leg

With A, ch 29 (33, 35). **Row 1 (RS)** Sc in 2nd ch from hook and in each ch across— 28 (32, 34) sts. Ch 1, turn. Beg with 2nd A row, cont in stripe pat II and inc 1 st each side on next row, then every 3rd row 10 (11, 12) times more—50 (56, 60) sts. Work even until piece measures 7 (8, 9)"/17.5 (20.5, 23)cm from beg. Fasten off. Turn work.

Crotch shaping

Next row Sk first 2 sts, join color in progress with a sc in next st, work across to within last 2 sts. Ch 1, turn—46 (52, 56) sts. Dec 1 st each side every row 3 times— 40 (46, 50) sts. Work even until piece measures 15 (16½, 18)"/38 (42, 45.5)cm from beg. Fasten off.

RIGHT LEG

Work as for left leg.

FINISHING

Sew front, back and leg seams. Measure waist and add 1"/2.5cm. Cut elastic to measurement. For casing for elastic, fold top edge of pants ¾"/2cm to WS and sew in place leaving a 1"/2.5cm opening at center back. Insert elastic through casing. Sew ends of elastic tog. Sew opening closed.

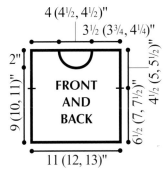

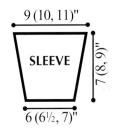

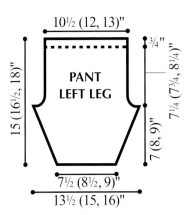

SIZES

Instructions are written for size 6 months. Changes for sizes 12 months and 18 months are in parentheses.

FINISHED MEASUREMENTS

Vest
• Chest (closed) 20 (22, 24)"/51 (56, 61)cm
• Length 10 (11, 12)"/25.5 (28, 30.5)cm

Hat
• Circumference 15"/38cm

MATERIALS

• 1 1³/₄oz/50g balls (each approx 152yd/139m) of Cleckheaton/Plymouth Yarns Angora Supreme (lambswool/angora) each in #7 dark purple (A), #3 lavender (B), #5 turquoise (C), #6 dark pink (D) and #4 medium pink (E) (4)
• 1 1³/₄oz/50g ball (approx 90yd/83m) of Berroco, Inc. Plush (nylon) in #1901 crema (F) (5)
• Size H/8 (5mm) crochet hook or size to obtain gauge

GAUGES

• 12 sts and 10 rows to 4"/10cm over hdc using size H/8 (5mm) hook.
• One granny square to 3³/₄"/9.5cm using size H/8 (5mm) hook.
Take time to check gauges.

NOTES

1) Body is worked in one piece to armhole, then both fronts and back are worked separately to shoulder.
2) See page 130 for working color changes for rows.

PATTERN STITCH

Row 1 (WS) Hdc in first 2 (3, 2) sts, *in next st work (yo, draw up a lp, yo, draw through 2 lps on hook) 3 times, yo and draw through all 4 lps on hook (bobble made), hdc in next 3 sts; rep from *, end bobble in next st, hdc in last 1 (2, 1) sts. Join C, ch 1, turn.
Row 2 Sc in each st across. Join D, ch 2, turn.
Rows 3 and 4 Hdc in each st across. Ch 2, turn. After row 4 is completed, join E, ch 3, turn.
Row 5 *Dc in next 2 sts, dc between next 2 sts of row below; rep from * to end. Join A, ch 2, turn.
Rows 6 and 7 Hdc in each st across. Ch 2, turn. After row 7 is completed, join B, ch 2, turn.
Rows 8 and 9 Hdc in each st across. Ch 2, turn. After row 9 is completed, join D, ch 2, turn.
Row 10 Hdc in each st across. Join E, ch 2, turn.
Row 11 Hdc in each st across. Join A, ch 2, turn.
Row 12 Hdc in each st across. Join B, ch 2, turn.
Rep rows 1-12 for pat st.

BODY

With A, ch 62 (68, 74). **Foundation row (RS)** Hdc in 3rd ch from hook and in each ch across—60 (66, 72) sts. Join B, ch 2, turn. Cont in pat st and work even until piece measures 6½ (7, 7½)"/16.5 (17.5, 19)cm from beg, end with a WS row.

Right front

Next row (RS) Work across first 12 (13, 14) sts. Keeping to pat st, ch and turn. Work even until armhole measures 1"/2.5cm, end with a WS row.

Neck shaping

Next row (RS) Dec 1 st at beg of row, then at same edge every row 5 (6, 7) times more—6 sts. Work even until armhole measures 3½ (4, 4½)"/9 (10, 11.5)cm. Fasten off.

Back

Next row (RS) Sk next 6 (7, 8) sts, join color in progress with a hdc in next st, then cont in pat st across next 23 (25, 27) sts. Keeping to pat st, ch and turn—24 (26, 28) sts. Work even until back measures same length as right front. Fasten off.

Left front

Next row (RS) Sk next 6 (7, 8) sts, join color in progress with a hdc in next st, then cont in pat st across last 11 (12, 13) sts. Keeping to pat st, ch and turn—12 (13, 14) sts. Cont to work same as right front, reversing neck shaping.

FINISHING

From RS, sc shoulders tog using E.

Trim

Trim is worked in chain st. Take care to maintain st and row gauge as you work. Position vest so bottom edge of left front is at top and RS is facing you. Make a slip

knot in end of F. Insert hook between first and 2nd sts on bottom edge. On WS, place slip knot on hook and draw up to RS. Insert hook between 2nd and 3rd sts and draw up a lp, then draw through lp on hook—first chain st made. Insert hook between 3rd and 4th sts and draw up a lp, then draw through lp on hook—2nd chain st made. Working from right to left, cont in chain st around entire outer edge. Fasten off.

Armhole trim

Beg at side seam, work chain st same as above.

Ties

(make 4)

With D, make a ch that measures 6"/15cm-long. Fasten off leaving a long tail for sewing. Sew first pair of ties at beg of neck shaping and 2nd pair 2¹/₂"/6.5cm below.

HAT

Basic Granny Square

Ch 4. Join ch with a sl st forming a ring.

Rnd 1 (RS) Ch 3 (always counts as 1 dc), work 2 dc over ring, ch 2, *work 3 dc over ring, ch 2; rep from * 3 times. Join rnd with a sl st in 3rd ch of ch-3. Fasten off. From WS, join next color with a sl st in any ch-2 sp.

Rnd 2 Ch 3, work 2 dc in same ch-2 sp, ch 1, *work (3 dc, ch 2, 3 dc) in next ch-2 sp, ch 1; rep from * 3 times, end with 3 dc in beg ch-2 sp, ch 2. Join rnd with a sl st in 3rd ch of ch-3. Fasten off. From RS, join next color with a sl st in any ch-2 sp.

Rnd 3 Ch 3, work 2 dc in same ch-2 sp, ch 1, *work 3 dc in next ch-1 sp, ch 1, work (3 dc, ch 2, 3 dc) in next ch-2 sp, ch 1; rep from * 3 times, end with 3 dc in next ch-1 sp, ch 1, 3 dc in beg ch-2 sp, ch 2. Join rnd with a sl st in 3rd ch of ch-3. Fasten off. From WS, join next color with a sl st in any ch-2 sp.

Rnd 4 Ch 1 (counts as 1 sc), work 2 sc in same ch-2 sp, cont to sc in each st around, working 3 sc in each corner. Join rnd with a sl st in ch-1. Fasten off leaving a long tail for sewing.

Brim

Make 4 basic granny squares in the following color combinations: **Square 1** Rnd 1 C, rnd 2 B, rnd 3 D and rnd 4 A. **Square 2** Rnd 1 D, rnd 2 B, rnd 3 A and rnd 4 E. **Square 3** Rnd 1 B, rnd 2 E, rnd 3 D and rnd 4 A. **Square 4** Rnd 1 E, rnd 2 A, rnd 3 B and rnd 4 D. Working through back lps, sew squares tog forming a ring.

Top edging

From RS, join D with a sc in any st. **Rnd 1** Sc in each st around. Join rnd with a sl st in first st. Fasten off.

Bottom edging

From RS, join E with a sc in any st. **Rnd 1** Sc in each st around. Join rnd with a sl st in first st. Fasten off.

CROWN

With E, ch 4. Join ch with a sl st forming a ring.

Rnd 1 (RS) Ch 3 (always counts as 1 dc), work 2 dc over ring, ch 2, *work 3 dc over ring, ch 2; rep from * 3 times. Join rnd with a sl st in 3rd ch of ch-3. Fasten off. From WS, join D with a sl st in any ch-2 sp.

Rnd 2 Ch 3, work 2 dc in same ch-2 sp, ch 1, *work (3 dc, ch 2, 3 dc) in next ch-2 sp, ch 1; rep from * 3 times, end with 3 dc in beg ch-2 sp, ch 2. Join rnd with a sl st in 3rd ch of ch-3. Fasten off. From RS, join A with a sl st in any ch-2 sp.

Rnd 3 Ch 1 (counts as 1 sc), work 2 sc in same ch-2 sp, cont to sc in each st around, working 3 sc in each corner. Join rnd with a sl st in ch-1. From WS, join C with a sl st in any corner st.

Rnd 4 Rep rnd 3. From RS, join B with a sl st in any corner st.

Rnd 5 Rep rnd 3. Fasten off leaving a long tail for sewing.

EAR FLAPS

With C, ch 5. **Row 1 (WS)** Sc in 2nd ch from hook and in next 2 ch, work 2 sc in last ch. Turn to bottom lps of beg ch, sc in next 4 lps—9 sts. Join B, ch 1, turn. **Row 2** Sc in first 4 sts, work 3 sc in next st (corner made), sc in last 4 sts. Join A, ch 1, turn.
Row 3 Sc in each st around, working 3 sc in center st of corner. Join E, ch 1, turn.
Row 4 Rep row 3. Join D, ch 1, turn. **Row 5** Rep row 3. Join C, ch 1, turn. **Row 6** Rep row 3. Join B, ch 1, turn. **Row 7** Rep row 3. Join A, ch 1, turn. **Row 8** Rep row 8. Fasten off. Turn to straight edge of earflap. From RS, join D with a sc in top right edge. **Row 1** Making sure that work lies flat, sc evenly across. Join E, ch 1, turn. **Row 2** Sc in each st across. Join B, ch 1, turn. **Row 3** Rep row 2. Fasten off.

FINISHING

Working through back lps, sew crown to brim.

Hat edging

From RS, join F with a sc in any st at bottom edge of brim. **Rnd 1** Sc in each st around. Join rnd with a sl st in first st. Fasten off.

Ear flap edging

From RS, join F with a sc in right bottom edge. **Row 1** Making sure that work lies flat, sc evenly around to left bottom edge. Fasten off.

Seam trim

Trim is worked in chain st. Take care to maintain gauge as you work. Position hat so crown/brim seam is at top and RS is facing you. Make a slip knot in end of F. Insert hook between first and 2nd sts to the left of one seam. On WS, place slip knot on hook and draw up to RS. Insert hook between 2nd and 3rd sts and draw up a lp, then draw through lp on hook—first chain st made. Insert hook between

3rd and 4th sts and draw up a lp, then draw through lp on hook—2nd chain st made. Working from right to left, cont in chain st around entire seam. Fasten off. Working in the same manner, work chain st along each seam of brim. Sew on ear flaps.

Ties

(make 2)

Cut one 13"/33cm-length each of A, B, C and E, and 2 lengths of D. Knot strands tog at one end. Braid strands, then knot opposite end. Sew ties to WS of ear flaps.

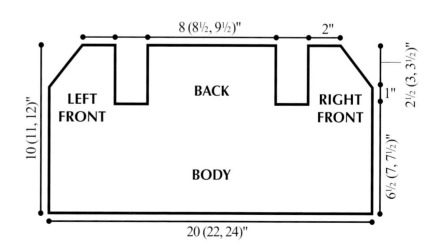

SIZES

Instructions are written for size 6 months. Changes for sizes 12 months and 18 months are in parentheses.

FINISHED MEASUREMENTS

- Chest 22 (24, 26)"/56 (61, 66)cm
- Length 11 (12, 13)"/28 (30.5, 33)cm
- Upper arm 9 (10, 10)"/23 (25.5, 25.5)cm

MATERIALS

- *3 (4, 4) 1³/₄oz/50g balls (each approx 122yd/113m) of Rowan Yarns Wool Cotton (wool/cotton) in #909 navy (MC)* **3**
- *1 (1, 2) balls in #901 citron (A)*
- *1 ball in #949 aqua (B)*
- *Size G/6 (4mm) crochet hook or size to obtain gauge*
- *Two bobbins*
- *Small safety pin*

GAUGE

15 sts and 12 rows to 4"/10cm over hdc using size G/6 (4mm) hook.
Take time to check gauge.

NOTES

1) See page 130 for working color changes.
2) Wind A onto 2 bobbins.

BACK

With MC, ch 36 (40, 44). **Row 1 (RS)** Hdc in 3rd ch from hook and in each ch across—34 (38, 42) sts. Ch 2, turn. **Row 2** Hdc in each st across. Ch 2, turn. Rep row 2 for pat st and work even until piece measures 11 (12, 13)"/28 (30.5, 33)cm from beg. Fasten off.

FRONT

With A, ch 8, change to MC and ch 34 (38, 42), change to another bobbin of A and ch 10. **Row 1 (RS)** With A, hdc in 3rd ch from hook and in next 7 ch, with MC, hdc in next 34 (38, 42) ch, with A, hdc in last 8 ch—50 (54, 58) sts. With A, ch 2, turn. **Row 2** With A, hdc in first 8 sts, with MC, hdc in next 34 (38, 42) sts, with A, hdc in last 8 sts. With A, ch 2, turn. Rep row 2 for pat st and color pat and work even until piece measures 6¹/₂ (7, 8)"/16.5 (17.5, 20.5)cm from beg, end with a WS row. Fasten off. Turn work.

Armhole shaping

Next row (RS) Sk first 8 sts, join MC with a hdc in next st, work across to within last 8 sts. With MC, ch 2, turn—34 (38, 42) sts. Cont with MC only and work even until armhole measures 1¹/₂"/4cm, end with a WS row.

Left neck shaping

Next row (RS) Work across first 17 (19, 21) sts, ch 2, turn. Dec 1 st from neck edge every row 7 (8, 8) times—10 (11, 13) sts. Work even until same length as back. Fasten off.

Right neck shaping

Next row (RS) Join MC with a hdc in next st, work to end. Cont to work as for left neck, reversing shaping.

SLEEVES

With B, ch 24 (26, 28). **Row 1 (RS)** Hdc in 3rd ch from hook and in each ch across—22 (24, 26) sts. Change to A, ch 2, turn. **Row 2** With A, hdc in first 4 sts, with MC, hdc in next 14 (16, 18) sts, with another bobbin of A, hdc last 4 sts. With A, ch 2, turn. Keeping 4 sts each side in A, inc 1 st each side of MC section on next row, then every 3rd row 5 (6, 5) times more—34 (38, 38) sts. Work even until piece measures 7 (8, 9)"/17.5 (20.5, 23)cm from beg, end with a WS row. Change to B, ch 2, turn. **Next row (RS)** With A, hdc in first 4 sts, with B, hdc in next 26 (30, 30) sts, with A, hdc last 4 sts. Fasten off.

FINISHING

Sew shoulder, side and sleeve seams. Set in sleeves matching A stripes at underarms.

Neck edging

From RS, join MC with a sl st in left shoulder seam. **Rnd 1** Ch 1, making sure that work lies flat, sc to center of v shaping, sc in center, mark this st with the safety pin, cont to sc around remaining neck edge. Join rnd with a sl st in first st. Change to B. **Rnd 2** Ch 2, hdc in each st to within one st of mark st; remove safety pin. To dec across 3 sts, work as foll: [Yo, draw up a lp in next st] 3 times, yo and draw through all lps on hook. Cont to hdc in each st to end. Join rnd with a sl st in first st. Change to MC. **Rnd 3** Ch 1, working through back lps only, sc in each st around. Join rnd with a sl st in first st. Fasten off.

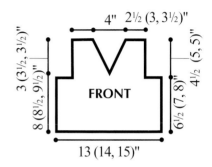

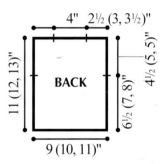

SIZES

Instructions are written for size 6 months. Changes for sizes 12 months and 18 months are in parentheses.

FINISHED MEASUREMENTS

• Chest (buttoned) 22 (24, 26)"/56 (61, 66)cm
• Hips 26 (28, 31)"/66 (71, 78.5)cm
• Length 21 (25, 27½)"/53.5 (63.5, 70)cm
• Upper arm 9 (10, 11)"/23 (25.5, 28)cm

MATERIALS

• 3 (4, 4) 1¾oz/50g skeins (each approx 108yd/100m) of Tahki Yarns/Tahki•Stacy Charles, Inc. Cotton Classic (cotton) each in #3003 ecru (A) and #3911 fuchsia (B)
• 1 skein in #3411 orange (C)
• Size G/6 (4mm) crochet hook or size to obtain gauge
• Five ⅝"16mm buttons

GAUGE

15 sts and 20 rows to 4"/10cm over sc using size G/6 (4mm) hook.
Take time to check gauge.

NOTE

See page 130 for working color changes for rows.

STRIPE PATTERN

Working in sc, work 6 rows A and 6 rows B. Rep these 12 rows for stripe pat.

LEFT LEG

With C, ch 27 (31, 35). **Row 1 (RS)** Sc in 2nd ch from hook and in each ch across—26 (30, 34) sts. Ch 1, turn. **Row 2** Sc in each st across. Ch 1, turn. Rep row 2 for pat st and work even for 2 more rows. Cont in stripe pat and inc 1 st each side on next row, then every other row 14 (14, 15) times more—56 (60, 66) sts. Work even until piece measures 7 (8, 9)"/17.5 (20.5, 23)cm from beg. Fasten off. Turn work.

Crotch shaping

Next row Sk first 2 sts, join color in progress with a sc in next st, work across to within last 2 sts. Ch 1, turn—52 (56, 62) sts. Dec 1 st each side every row twice—48 (52, 58) sts. Work one more row if necessary to end with a WS row. Fasten off.

RIGHT LEG

Work as for left leg. Sew front, back and leg seams.

BODY

From RS, join color in progress with a sc in first st, then sc in each st across—96 (104, 116) sts. Cont in stripe pat as established until piece measures 12 (14, 16)"/30.5 (35.5, 40.5)cm from beg, end with a WS row.

Waist shaping

Next row (RS) Sc in first 22 (24, 27) sts, [dec 1 st over next 2 sts] twice, sc in next 44 (48, 54) sts, [dec 1 st over next 2 sts] twice, sc in last 22 (24, 27) sts—92 (100, 112) sts. Work 3 rows even. **Next row (RS)** Sc in first 21 (23, 26) sts, [dec 1 st over next 2 sts] twice, sc in next 42 (46, 52) sts, [dec 1 st over next 2 sts] twice, sc in last 21 (23, 26) sts—88 (96, 108) sts. Work 3 rows even. **Next row (RS)** Sc in first 20 (22, 25) sts, [dec 1 st over next 2 sts] twice, sc in next 40 (44, 50) sts, [dec 1 st over next 2 sts] twice, sc in last 20 (22, 25) sts—84 (92, 104) sts. Work 0 (3, 3) rows even.

For sizes 18 and 24 months only
Next row (RS) Sc in first 22 (24) sts, [dec 1 st over next 2 sts] 1 (2) times, sc in next 44 (48) sts, [dec 1 st over next 2 sts] 1 (2) times, sc in last 22 (24) sts—90 (100) sts.
For all sizes
Work even on 84 (90, 100) sts until piece measures 16$\frac{1}{2}$ (20, 22)"/42 (51, 56)cm from beg, end with a WS row. Mark last row for beg of armhole.

RIGHT FRONT
Next row (RS) Work across first 19 (20, 23) sts. Ch 1, turn. Work even until armhole measures 2$\frac{1}{2}$ (2$\frac{1}{2}$, 3)"/6.5 (6.5, 7.5)cm, end with a RS row.
Neck shaping
Next row (WS) Work across to within last 2 sts. Ch 1, turn. Dec 1 st at beg of next row, then at same edge every row 3 (3, 4) times more—13 (14, 16) sts. Work even until armhole measures 4$\frac{1}{2}$ (5, 5$\frac{1}{2}$)"/11.5 (12.5, 14)cm. Fasten off.

BACK
Next row (RS) Sk next 4 sts, join color in progress with a sc in next st, sc across next 37 (41, 45) sts. Ch 1, turn—38 (42, 46) sts.

Work even until back measures same length as right front. Fasten off.

LEFT FRONT
Next row (RS) Sk next 4 sts, join color in progress with a sc in next st, sc to end. Ch 1, turn—19 (20, 23) sts. Cont to work same as for right front, reversing neck shaping.

SLEEVES
With C, ch 25 (27, 29). **Row 1 (RS)** Sc in 2nd ch from hook and in each ch across—24 (26, 28) sts. Ch 1, turn. Work in sc for 3 more rows. Join A, ch 1, turn. Cont in stripe pat and inc 1 st each side on next row, then every 4th row 4 (5, 6) times more—34 (38, 42) sts. Work even until piece measures 7$\frac{1}{2}$ (8$\frac{1}{2}$, 9)"/19 (21.5, 23)cm from beg. Fasten off.

FINISHING
Sew shoulder seams. Sew front crotch seam for 4 (5, 6)"/10 (12.5, 15)cm.
Front and neck bands
With RS of right front facing, join C with a sc above crotch seam. **Row 1** Making sure that work lies flat, sc evenly up right front

edge, around neck edge, then down left front edge, working 3 sc in each corner st. Ch 1, turn. **Row 2** Sc in each st across, working 3 sc in each corner st. Ch 1, turn. Place markers on right front band for 5 buttons, with the first 2 sts from neck edge, the last 1"/2.5cm from top of crotch seam and the rest spaced evenly between. **Row 3 (buttonhole row)** *Sc in each st to marker, ch 2, sk next 2 sts; rep from * 5 times, then cont in sc to end, working 3 sc in each corner st. Ch 1, turn. **Row 4** Sc in each st across, working 2 sc in each ch-2 sp. Fasten off. Lap right front band over left and sew bottom edges of bands in place.

Collar

From RS, join C with a sc 1"/2.5cm from right front edge, sc in each st across to within 1"/2.5cm of left front edge. Ch 1, turn. Work in sc and inc 1 st each side on next row, then every other row twice more. Work even until collar measures 2½ (3, 3)"/6.5 (7.5, 7.5)cm from beg. Fasten off. Sew sleeve seams. Set in sleeves. Sew on buttons.

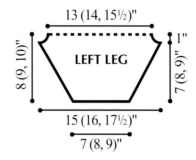

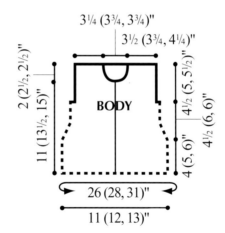

SIZES

Instructions are written for size 6 months. Changes for sizes 12 months and 18 months are in parentheses.

FINISHED MEASUREMENTS

• Chest (closed) 22 (24, 26)"/56 (61, 66)cm
• Length 11 (12, 13)"/28 (30.5, 33)cm
• Upper arm 8 (9, 10)"/20.5 (23, 25.5)cm

MATERIALS

• 3 (4, 5) 3oz/85g skeins (each approx 174yd/157m) of Lion Brand Yarn Co. Lion Chenille (acrylic) in #600 black 〔5〕
• Size H/8 (5mm) crochet hook or size to obtain gauge
• ¹/₂yd/.5m of Asian print magenta satin fabric
• Two small black frog fasteners
• Matching sewing threads
• Sewing needle
• Straight pins

GAUGE

12 sts and 12 rows to 4"/10cm over hdc using size H/8 (5mm) hook.
Take time to check gauge.

BACK

Ch 36 (38, 42). **Row 1 (RS)** Hdc in 3rd ch from hook and in each ch across—34 (36, 40) sts. Ch 2, turn. **Row 2** Hdc in each st across. Ch 2, turn. Rep row 2 for pat st and work even until piece measures 7 (7¹/₂, 8)"/17.5 (19, 20.5)cm from beg, end with a WS row. Fasten off. Turn work.

Armhole shaping

Next row (RS) Sk first 3 sts, join yarn with a hdc in next st, work to within last 3 sts. Ch 2, turn—28 (30, 34) sts. Work even until armhole measures 4 (4¹/₂, 5)"/10 (11.5, 12.5)cm. Fasten off.

LEFT FRONT

Ch 24 (26, 28). **Row 1 (RS)** Hdc in 3rd ch from hook and in each ch across—22 (24, 26) sts. Ch 2, turn. Work even in hdc until piece measures 7 (7¹/₂, 8)"/17.5 (19, 20.5)cm from beg, end with a WS row. Fasten off. Turn work.

Armhole and neck shaping

Next row (RS) Sk first 3 sts, join yarn with a hdc in next st, work across to within last 3 sts. Ch 2, turn—16 (18, 20) sts.

Neck shaping

Next row (WS) Dec 1 st at beg of row, then at same edge every row 6 (8, 9) times more—9 (9, 10) sts. Work even until same length as back. Fasten off.

RIGHT FRONT

Work as for left front, reversing shaping.

SLEEVES

Ch 20 (22, 24). **Row 1 (RS)** Hdc in 3rd ch from hook and in each ch across—18 (20, 22) sts. Ch 2, turn. Work in hdc and inc 1 st each side on next row, then every 4th row 2 (3, 3) times more—24 (28, 30) sts. Work even until piece measures 8 (9, 10)"/20.5(23, 25.5)cm from beg. Fasten off.

FINISHING

Sew shoulder seams. Set in sleeves, sewing last 1"/2.5cm at top of sleeve to armhole sts. Sew side and sleeve seams.

Fabric trim

For fronts, necks and bottom edges, cut two strips of fabric 2"/5cm-wide by 31 (36, 42)"/78.5 (91.5, 106.5)cm-long. Sew short ends tog using a ¹/₂"/13mm seam; press seam open. Fold fabric strip in half lengthwise, WS facing; press. Fold each long edge ¹/₄"/6mm to WS; press. Center seam at center back neck. Taking care to maintain st and row gauges, pin trim around entire edge, mitering trim around corners and ending at center back bottom. Trim excess fabric, leaving a 2"/5cm overlap. Fold each short edge 1"/2.5cm to WS, then overlap edges 1"/2.5cm. Working through all thicknesses, sew trim along top folded edges.

For cuffs, cut two strips of fabric 2"/5cm-wide by 8 (8¹/₂, 9)"/20.5 (21.5, 17.5)cm-long. Fold and press fabric strips same as for edging. Beg and ending at underarm seam, sew trim to sleeves. Sew on frogs.

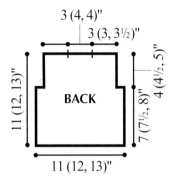

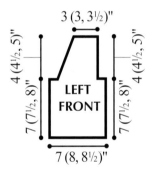

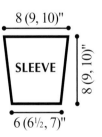

SIZES

Instructions are written for size 6 months. Changes for sizes 12 months and 18 months are in parentheses.

FINISHED MEASUREMENTS

• Chest 20 (22, 24)"/51 (56, 61)cm

MATERIALS

• 2 1³/₄oz/50g skeins (each approx 136yd/125m) of Berroco, Inc. Cotton Twist (cotton/rayon) in #8347 frankenberry (MC) **4**
• 1 3oz/85g skeins (each approx 174yd/157m) of Lion Brand Yarn Co. Lion Chenille Sensations (acrylic) in #600 black (CC) **5**
• Size H/8 (5mm) crochet hook or size to obtain gauge
• 1yd/1m of Asian print magenta satin fabric
• Two small black frog fasteners
• Matching sewing threads
• Sewing needle
• Straight pins

GAUGE

14 sts and 16 rows to 4"/10cm over pat st using size H/8 (5mm) hook.
Take time to check gauge.

PATTERN STITCH

Row 1 Working through front lps only, sc in each st across. Ch 1, turn.
Rep row 1 for pat st.

BACK BODICE

With MC, ch 33 (37, 41). **Foundation row (RS)** Sc in 2nd ch from hook and in each ch across—32 (36, 40) sts. Ch 1, turn. Cont in pat st and work even until piece measures 2¹/₂ (3, 3¹/₂)"/6.5 (7.5, 9)cm from beg, end with a WS row. Fasten off. Turn work.

Armhole shaping

Next row (RS) Sk first 3 sts, join MC with a sc in front lp of next st, work to within last 3 sts. Ch 1, turn—26 (30, 34) sts. Work even until armhole measures 3 (3¹/₂, 4)"/2.5 (4, 5)cm. Fasten off.

LEFT FRONT BODICE

With MC, ch 23 (25, 27). **Foundation row (RS)** Sc in 2nd ch from hook and in each ch across—22 (24, 26) sts. Ch 1, turn. Cont in pat st for 2 rows, end with a RS row.

Neck shaping

Next row (WS) Dec 1 st at beg of row, then at same edge every other row 10 (11, 11) times more. AT SAME TIME, when piece measures 2¹/₂ (3, 3¹/₂)"/6.5 (7.5, 9)cm from beg, end with a WS row. Fasten off. Turn work.

Armhole shaping

Next row (RS) Sk first 3 sts, join MC with a sc in next st, work to end. Ch 1, turn. When neck shaping has been completed, work even on 8 (9, 11) sts until same length as back. Fasten off.

RIGHT FRONT BODICE

With MC, ch 23 (25, 27). **Foundation row (RS)** Sc in 2nd ch from hook and in each ch across—22 (24, 26) sts. Ch 1, turn. Cont in pat st and work even until piece measures $2\frac{1}{2}$ (3, $3\frac{1}{2}$)"/6.5 (7.5, 9)cm from beg, end with a WS row.

Armhole shaping

Next row (RS) Work across to within last 3 sts. Ch 1, turn—19 (21, 23) sts.

Neck shaping

Next row (WS) Dec 1 st at end of row, then at same edge every row 10 (11, 11) times more—8 (9, 11) sts. Work even until same length as back. Fasten off.

FINISHING

Sew shoulder and side seams.

Edging

Lap right front over left front. On left front, use straight pins to mark where right front overlaps at neck and at bottom edge. Lift off right front. Move neck pin 2"/5cm down towards bottom edge and bottom pin 1"/2.5cm towards front edge. From RS, join CC with a sc at pin mark on left front bottom edge. Making sure that work lies flat, sc evenly around outer edge, working 2 sc in each corner and ending at pin mark on left front neck edge. Fasten off. Lap right front over left front and tack bottom edges tog where they overlap.

Armhole edging

From RS, join CC with a sc in underarm seam. **Rnd 1** Ch 1, making sure that work lies flat, sc evenly around armhole edge. Join rnd with a sl st in first sc. Fasten off.

Skirt

Cut a 30 (32, 36)"/76 (81, 91.5)cm by 20 (22, 23)"/51 (56, 58.5)cm piece of fabric. With RS tog and using $\frac{1}{2}$"/13mm seam allowance, sew back seam. Gather one long edge of skirt, adjusting gathers to fit lower edge of bodice. Handsew skirt in place. Fold hem $\frac{1}{4}$"/6mm to WS; press. Hem skirt to desired length. Sew on frogs.

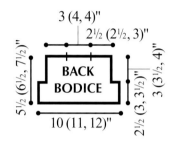

3 (4, 4)"
$2\frac{1}{2}$ ($2\frac{1}{2}$, 3)"
$5\frac{1}{2}$ ($6\frac{1}{2}$, $7\frac{1}{2}$)"
BACK BODICE
3 ($3\frac{1}{2}$, 4)"
$2\frac{1}{2}$ (3, $3\frac{1}{2}$)"
10 (11, 12)"
$2\frac{1}{2}$ (3, $3\frac{1}{2}$)"

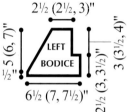

$2\frac{1}{2}$ ($2\frac{1}{2}$, 3)"
5 (6, 7)"
$\frac{1}{2}$"
LEFT BODICE
3 ($3\frac{1}{2}$, 4)"
$2\frac{1}{2}$ (3, $3\frac{1}{2}$)"
$6\frac{1}{2}$ (7, $7\frac{1}{2}$)"

$2\frac{1}{2}$ ($2\frac{1}{2}$, 3)"
3 ($3\frac{1}{2}$, 4)"
RIGHT BODICE
3 ($3\frac{1}{2}$, 4)"
$2\frac{1}{2}$ (3, $3\frac{1}{2}$)"
$6\frac{1}{2}$ (7, $7\frac{1}{2}$)"
$2\frac{1}{2}$ (3, $3\frac{1}{2}$)"

b l u e   d r e a m s

SIZES

Instructions are written for size 6 months. Changes for sizes 12 months and 18 months are in parentheses.

FINISHED MEASUREMENTS

• Chest (closed) 22 (24, 26)"/56 (61, 66)cm
• Length 11 (12, 13)"/28 (30.5, 33)cm
• Upper arm 9 (10, 11)"/23 (25.5, 28)cm

MATERIALS

• 3 (4, 4) 1³/₄oz/50g balls (each approx 137yd/125m) of Filatura Di Crosa/Tahki•Stacy Charles, Inc. Zara (wool) in #1481 denim blue (MC) ③
• 1 1³/₄oz/50g ball (approx 55yd/50m) of Filatura Di Crosa/Tahki•Stacy Charles, Inc. Yogi (wool/acrylic/polymide) in #57 honey bear (CC) ⑤
• Size H/8 and I/9 (5 and 5.5mm) crochet hooks or size to obtain gauge
• Two skeins of DMC Six-Strand Embroidery Floss in #742 dark yellow
• Embroidery needle
• Straight pins

GAUGE

14 sts and 17 rows to 4"/10cm over sc using smaller hook.
Take time to check gauge.

NOTE

It's sometimes difficult seeing the sts when working with furry yarn. For best results, count sts as you work across each row to make sure you do not skip or miss a st.

BACK

With smaller hook and MC, ch 39 (43, 47). **Row 1 (RS)** Sc in 2nd ch from hook and in each ch across—38 (42, 46) sts. Ch 1, turn. **Row 2** Sc in each st across. Ch 1, turn. Rep row 2 for pat st and work even until piece measures 6¹/₂ (7, 7¹/₂)"/16.5 (17.5, 19)cm from beg, end with a WS row. Fasten off. Turn work.

Armhole shaping

Next row (RS) Sk first 4 sts, join MC with a sc in next st, work across to within last 4 sts. Ch 1, turn—30 (34, 38) sts. Work even until armhole measures 4 (4¹/₂, 5)"/10 (11.5, 12.5)cm, end with a WS row.

Left neck shaping

Next row (RS) Work across first 8 (9, 10) sts, ch 1, turn. Work one more row; piece should measure 11 (12, 13)"/28 (30.5, 33)cm from beg. Fasten off.

Right neck shaping

Next row (RS) Sk 14 (16, 18) center sts, join MC with a sc in next st, work to end. Ch 1, turn. Work one more row. Fasten off.

LEFT FRONT

With smaller hook and MC, ch 21 (23, 25). **Row 1 (RS)** Sc in 2nd ch from hook and in each ch across—20 (22, 24) sts. Ch 1, turn. Work even in sc until piece measures 6½ (7, 7½)"/16.5 (17.5, 19)cm from beg, end with a WS row. Fasten off. Turn work.

Armhole shaping

Next row (RS) Sk first 4 sts, join MC with a sc in next st, work to end. Ch 1, turn— 16 (18, 20) sts. Work even until armhole measures 2½ (2½, 3)"/6.5 (6.5, 7.5)cm, end with a WS row.

Neck shaping

Next row (RS) Work across first 13 (14, 15) sts. Ch 1, turn. Dec 1 st at neck edge on next row, then every row 4 times more—8 (9, 10) sts. Work even until same length as back. Fasten off.

RIGHT FRONT

Work as for left front reversing shaping.

SLEEVES

With smaller hook and MC, ch 23 (24, 26). **Row 1 (RS)** Sc in 2nd ch from hook and in each ch across—22 (23, 25) sts. Ch 1, turn. Work in sc and inc 1 st each side on next row, then every 4th row 4 (5, 6) times more—32 (35, 39) sts. Work even until piece measures 7 (8, 9)"/17.5 (20.5, 23)cm from beg. Fasten off.

POCKET FLAPS

(make 2)
Beg at bottom edge, with smaller hook and MC, ch 2. **Row 1 (RS)** Work 3 sc in 2nd ch from hook—3 sts. Ch 1, turn. Working in sc, inc 1 st each side on next row, then every row twice more—9 sts. Work even until piece measures 2"/5cm from beg. Fasten off.

blue dreams

FINISHING

Sew shoulder seams. Set in sleeves, sewing last 1"/2.5cm at top of sleeve to armhole sts. Sew side and sleeve seams.

Edging

With RS facing and smaller hook, join MC with a sc in left shoulder seam. **Rnd 1** Making sure that work lies flat, sc evenly around neck, front and bottom edges, working 3 sc in each corner. Join rnd with a sl st in first st. **Rnd 2** Ch 1, working through back lps only, sc in each st around, working 3 sc in each corner st. Join rnd with a sl st in first st. Fasten off.

Left front band

With RS facing and smaller hook, join MC with a sc in bottom side edge. **Row 1** Working through back lps only, sc in each st to beg of neck. Fasten off.

Right front band

With RS facing and smaller hook, join MC with a sc in side edge of neck. **Row 1** Working through back lps only, sc in each st to bottom edge. Fasten off.

Embroidery

Use all six-strands of floss in needle throughout and refer to photo. For stitching detail around edge, beg at top left neck edge. Working between rows 1 and 2 of edging, sew running stitches (going under one st and over one st) down left front, along bottom, then up right front to top neck edge. For horizontal line of stitching on left front, measure $1/2$ ($1/2$, 1)"/1.3 (1.3, 2.5)cm from beg of armhole. Sew running stitches from armhole edge to stitching along front edge. Position a pocket flap on left front, so top edge is even with horizontal line of sts and side edge of pocket flap is 1"/2.5cm from side edge of armhole; pin in place. Sew pocket flap in place using running stitches; as shown. For vertical stitching lines for mock darts, beg each on side edges of pocket flap and stitch down to stitching line along bottom edge, tapering lines; as shown. Rep stitching lines on right front.

Collar

From RS, sk right front band, with larger hook join CC with a sc in right front neck. **Row 1** Sc in each st across neck to left front band. Ch 3, turn. **Row 2** Dc in each st across. Ch 1, turn. **Row 3** Sc in each st across. Fasten off.

Cuffs

With larger hook and CC, ch 18 (20, 21). **Row 1** Hdc in 3rd ch from hook and in each ch across—16 (18, 19) sts. **Row 2** Work 2 hdc in first st, hdc in each st to within last st, work 2 hdc in last st—18 (20, 21) sts. Ch 2, turn. **Rows 3 and 4** Hdc in each st across. Ch 2, turn. After row 4 is completed, do not ch, fasten off. Sew side seams. Sew cuffs onto sleeves.

Front and bottom trim

Trim is worked in chain st. Take care to maintain st and row gauge as you work. Position vest so bottom edge of left front is at top and RS is facing you. Make a slip knot in end of CC. Using larger hook, insert hook between first and 2nd sts on bottom edge. On WS, place slip knot on hook and draw up to RS. Insert hook between 2nd and 3rd sts and draw up a lp, then draw through lp on hook—first chain st made. Insert hook between 3rd and 4th sts and draw up a lp, then draw through lp on hook—2nd chain st made. Working from right to left, cont in chain st to top of right front band. Fasten off.

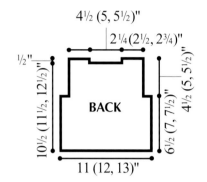

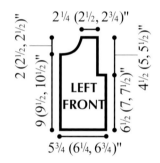

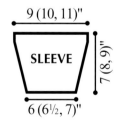

v e s t   f r i e n d

SIZES

Instructions are written for size 6 months. Changes for sizes 12 months and 18 months are in parentheses.

FINISHED MEASUREMENTS

• Chest (closed) 22 (24, 26)"/56 (61, 66)cm
• Length 11 (12, 13)"/28 (30.5, 33)cm

MATERIALS

• 2 (3, 3) 1³/₄oz/50g balls (each approx 137yd/125m) of Filatura Di Crosa/Tahki• Stacy Charles, Inc. Zara (wool) in #1481 denim blue (MC) **3**
• 1 1³/₄oz/50g ball (approx 55yd/50m) of Filatura Di Crosa/Tahki•Stacy Charles, Inc. Yogi (wool/acrylic/ polymide) in #57 honey bear (CC) **5**
• Size H/8 and I/9 (5 and 5.5mm) crochet hooks or size to obtain gauge
• Two skeins of DMC Six-Strand Embroidery Floss in #742 dark yellow
• Embroidery needle
• Straight pins

GAUGE

14 sts and 17 rows to 4"/10cm over sc using smaller hook and MC.
Take time to check gauge.

NOTE

It's sometimes difficult seeing the sts when working with furry yarn. For best results, count sts as you work across each row to make sure you do not skip or miss a st.

BACK

With smaller hook and MC, ch 39 (43, 47). **Row 1 (RS)** Sc in 2nd ch from hook and in each ch across—38 (42, 46) sts. Ch 1, turn. **Row 2** Sc in each st across. Ch 1, turn. Rep row 2 for pat st and work even until piece measures 6¹/₂ (7, 7¹/₂)"/16.5 (17.5, 19)cm from beg, end with a WS row. Fasten off. Turn work.

Armhole shaping

Next row (RS) Sk first 4 sts, join MC with a sc in next st, work across to within last 4 sts. Ch 1, turn—30 (34, 38) sts. Work even until armhole measures 4 (4¹/₂, 5)"/10 (11.5, 12.5)cm, end with a WS row.

Left neck shaping

Next row (RS) Work across first 8 (9, 10) sts, ch 1, turn. Work one more row; piece should measure 11 (12, 13)"/28 (30.5, 33)cm from beg. Fasten off.

Right neck shaping

Next row (RS) Sk 14 (16, 18) center sts, join MC with a sc in next st, work to end. Ch 1, turn. Work one more row. Fasten off.

LEFT FRONT

With smaller hook and MC, ch 21 (23, 25). **Row 1 (RS)** Sc in 2nd ch from hook and in each ch across—20 (22, 24) sts. Ch 1, turn. **Row 2** Sc in each st across. Ch 1, turn. Rep row 2 for pat st and work even until piece measures 6$\frac{1}{2}$ (7, 7$\frac{1}{2}$)"/16.5 (17.5, 19)cm from beg, end with a WS row. Fasten off. Turn work.

Armhole shaping

Next row (RS) Sk first 4 sts, join MC with a sc in next st, work to end. Ch 1, turn— 16 (18, 20) sts. Work even until armhole measures 2$\frac{1}{2}$ (3, 3)"/6.5 (7.5, 7.5)cm, end with a WS row.

Neck shaping

Next row (RS) Work across first 13 (14, 15) sts. Ch 1, turn. Dec 1 st at neck edge on next row, then every row 4 times more—8 (9, 10) sts. Work even until same length as back. Fasten off.

RIGHT FRONT

Work as for left front reversing shaping.

POCKET FLAPS

(make 2)

Beg at bottom edge, with smaller hook and MC, ch 2. **Row 1 (RS)** Work 3 sc in 2nd ch from hook—3 sts. Ch 1, turn. Working in sc, inc 1 st each side on next row, then every row twice more—9 sts. Work even until piece measures 2"/5cm from beg. Fasten off.

FINISHING

Sew shoulder and side seams.

Edging

With RS facing and smaller hook, join MC with a sc in left shoulder seam. **Rnd 1** Making sure that work lies flat, sc evenly around neck, front and bottom edges, working 3 sc in each corner. Join rnd with a sl st in first st. **Rnd 2** Ch 1, sc in each st around, working 3 sc in each corner st. Join rnd with a sl st in first st. Fasten off.

Left front band

With RS facing and smaller hook, join MC with a sc in bottom side edge. **Row 1** Sc in each st to beg of neck. Fasten off.

Right front band

With RS facing and smaller hook, join MC with a sc in side edge of neck. **Row 1** Sc in each st to bottom edge. Fasten off.

Embroidery

Use all six strands of floss in needle throughout and refer to photo. For stitching detail around edge, beg at top left neck edge. Working between rows 1 and 2 of edging, sew running stitches (going under one st and over one st) down left front, along bottom, then up right front to top neck edge. For horizontal line of stitching on left front, measure $\frac{1}{2}$ ($\frac{1}{2}$, 1)"/1.3 (1.3, 2.5)cm from beg of armhole. Sew running stitches from armhole edge to stitching along front edge. Position a pocket flap on left front, so top edge is even with horizontal line of sts and side edge of pocket flap is 1"/2.5cm from side edge of armhole; pin in place. Sew pocket flap in place using running stitches; as shown. For vertical stitching lines for mock darts, beg each one on side edges of pocket flap and stitch down to stitching line along bottom edge, tapering lines; as shown. Rep stitching lines on right front.

Collar

From RS, sk right front edging and band,

with larger hook join CC with a hdc in right front neck. **Row 1** Hdc in each st across to left front neck edge. Ch 2, turn. **Row 2** Work 2 hdc in first st, hdc in each st across to last st, work 2 hdc in last st. Ch 2, turn. Rep row 2 once more. Fasten off.

Front and bottom trim

Trim is worked in chain st. Take care to maintain st and row gauge as you work. Position vest so bottom edge of left front is at top and RS is facing you. Make a slip knot in end of CC. Using larger hook, insert hook between first and 2nd sts on bottom edge. On WS, place slip knot on hook and draw up to RS. Insert hook between 2nd and 3rd sts and draw up a lp, then draw through lp on hook—first chain st made. Insert hook between 3rd and 4th sts and draw up a lp, then draw through lp on hook—2nd chain st made. Working from right to left, cont in chain st to top of right front band. Fasten off.

Armhole trim

Beg at side seam, work chain st same as for front and bottom trim.

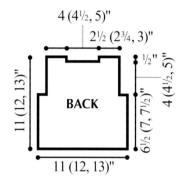

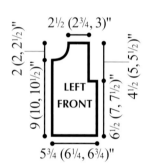

living color

SIZE

Instructions are written for size 6-18 months.

FINISHED MEASUREMENTS

• Width 24"/61cm
• Length 12"/30.5cm

MATERIALS

• 1oz/30g scraps of worsted weight yarns in bright pink (A), light pink (B), red (C), medium purple (D), lilac (E), light blue (F), dark blue (G), light teal (H) and dark teal (I) **4**
• 1oz/30g scrap of worsted weight fur yarn in cream (J) **5**
• Size H/8 (5mm) crochet hook or size to obtain gauge

GAUGE

12 sts and 9 rows to 4"/10cm over dc using size H/8 (5mm) hook.
Take time to check gauge.

STRIPE PATTERN

Work 1 rnd each using A, B, C, D, E, F, G, H, I and J.
Rep these 10 rnds for stripe pat.

PONCHO

Beg at neck edge, with A, ch 36. Taking care not to twist ch, join ch with a sl st forming a ring. **Rnd 1 (RS)** Ch 3 (counts as 1 dc), work 2 dc in same ch as joining (first corner made), dc in next 8 ch, [work 3 dc in next ch, dc in next 8 ch] 3 times. Join rnd with a sl st in 3rd ch of ch-3. Fasten off. **Rnd 2 (RS)** Join B with a dc in center st of any 3-dc corner, work 2 dc in same st (corner made), *dc in each st to center st of next 3-dc corner, work 3 dc in center st; rep from * around. Join rnd with a sl st in first st. Fasten off. Rep rnd 2 for pat st. Beg with C, cont to work stripe pat until 20 rnds have been completed or work to desired length.

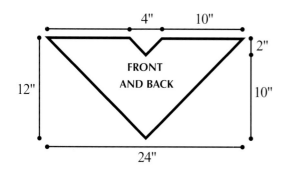

4"   10"

2"

FRONT
AND BACK

12"

10"

24"

g o l d e n   c h i l d

SIZES

Instructions are written for size 6 months. Changes for sizes 12 months and 18 months are in parentheses.

FINISHED MEASUREMENTS

- Chest (closed) 24 (26, 27½)"/61 (66, 70)cm
- Length 11 (12, 13)"/28 (30.5, 33)cm
- Upper arm 10 (11, 12)"/25.5 (28, 30.5)cm

MATERIALS

- 4 (5,5) 1¾oz/50g balls (each approx 120yd/110m) of Berroco, Inc. Suede (nylon) in #3714 Hopalong Cassidy (MC) **4**
- 1 1¾oz/50g ball (approx 90yd/83m) of Berroco, Inc. Plush (nylon) in #1901 crema (CC) **5**
- Size H/8 (5mm) crochet hook or size to obtain gauge
- Yarn needle
- 9 (10, 10½)"/23 (25.5, 26.5)cm-long separating zipper
- Matching sewing thread
- Sewing needle
- 2½"/6.5cm square piece of cardboard (for tassel)

GAUGE

14 sts and 17 rows to /10cm over sc using size H/8 (5mm) hook and MC.
Take time to check gauge.

NOTE

It's sometimes difficult seeing the sts when working with furry yarn. For best results, count sts as you work across each row to make sure you do not skip or miss a st.

BACK

With MC, ch 43 (47, 49). **Row 1 (WS)** Sc in 2nd ch from hook and in each ch across—42 (46, 48) sts. Ch 1, turn. **Row 2** Sc in each st across. Ch 1, turn. Rep row 2 for pat st and work even until piece measures 10½ (11½, 12½)"/26.5 (29, 31.5)cm from beg, end with a WS row.

Right neck shaping

Next row (RS) Work across first 15 (16, 17) sts, ch 1, turn. Work one more row; piece should measure 11 (12, 13)"/28 (30.5, 33)cm from beg. Fasten off.

Left neck shaping

Next row (RS) Sk 12 (14, 14) center sts, join MC with a sc in next st, work to end. Ch 1, turn. Work one more row. Fasten off.

LEFT FRONT

With MC, ch 22 (24, 25). **Row 1 (WS)** Sc in 2nd ch from hook and in each ch across— 21 (23, 24) sts. Ch 1, turn. Work even in sc until piece measures 9 (10, 10½")/23 (25.5, 26.5)cm from beg, end with a WS row.

Neck shaping

Next row (RS) Work across first 19 (20, 21) sts. Ch 1, turn. Dec 1 st at neck edge on next row, then every row 3 times more— 15 (16, 17) sts. Work even until same length as back. Fasten off.

RIGHT FRONT

Work as for left front reversing shaping.

SLEEVES

With MC, ch 22 (24, 27). **Row 1 (RS)** Sc in 2nd ch from hook and in each ch across— 21 (23, 26) sts. Ch 1, turn. Work in sc and inc 1 st each side on next row, then every 3rd row 6 (7, 7) times more—35 (39, 42) sts. Work even until piece measures 7 (8, 9)"/17.5 (20.5, 23)cm from beg. Fasten off.

g o l d e n   c h i l d

FINISHING

Sew shoulder seams. Place markers 5 (5$\frac{1}{2}$, 6)"/12.5 (14, 15)cm down from shoulder seams on fronts and back. Sew sleeves to armholes between markers. Sew side and sleeve seams.

Edging

With RS facing, join MC with a sc in left shoulder seam. **Rnd 1** Making sure that work lies flat, sc evenly around neck, fronts and bottom edges, working 3 sc in each corner. Join rnd with a sl st in first st. Fasten off.
For sleeves, join MC with a sc in sleeve seam. **Rnd 1** Making sure that work lies flat, sc evenly around bottom edge. Join rnd with a sl st in first st. Fasten off.

Front and bottom trim

With RS facing, join CC with a sc in top left front edge. **Row 1** Sc in each st around to top right front edge, working 3 sc in each corner. Ch 2, turn. **Row 2** Working in same MC st as row 1, hdc in each st around, working 2 hdc in center st of each corner. Fasten off.

Collar

From RS, sk first st of right front neck, join CC with a hdc in next st. **Row 1** Hdc in each st across neck to within last st of left front neck. Ch 2, turn. **Rows 2, 3 and 4** Work 2 hdc in first st, hdc in each st to within last st, work 2 hdc in last st. Ch 2, turn. **Row 5** Hdc in each st across. Fasten off.

Cuffs

From RS, join CC with a sl st in first st at sleeve seam. **Rnd 1** Ch 2, hdc in each st around. Join rnd with a sl st in first ch of ch-2. Ch 2, turn. **Rnd 2** Hdc in each st around, inc 2 sts evenly spaced. Join rnd with a sl st in first ch of ch-2. Ch 2, turn. **Rnds 3 and 4** Hdc in each st around. Join rnd with a sl st in first ch of ch-2. After rnd 4 is completed, do not ch, fasten off. Fold back cuffs.

Embroidery

Use one strand of CC in needle throughout and refer to photo. For stitching detail around sleeve, beg at underarm seam.

Working around last row of sleeve, sew running stitches (going under one st and over one st). For horizontal line of stitching on back, measure 1 (1½, 2)"/2.5 (4, 5)cm from beg of armhole. Sew running stitches from armhole edge to armhole edge. Rep horizontal lines on each front. Sew in zipper.

Tassel

Wrap MC 19 times around cardboard. Slip a 10"/25.5cm-length of MC under strands and tightly knot at one end of cardboard. Remove cardboard. Wrap and tie another length of yarn around the tassel about ½"/1.5cm down from the top. Cut loops at opposite ends. Trim ends even. Attach tassel to zipper pull.

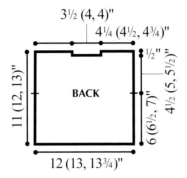

3½ (4, 4)"
4¼ (4½, 4¾)"
½"
11 (12, 13)"
BACK
4½ (5, 5½)"
6 (6½, 7)"
12 (13, 13¾)"

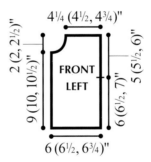

4¼ (4½, 4¾)"
5 (5½, 6)"
2 (2, 2½)"
9 (10, 10½)"
FRONT LEFT
6 (6½, 7)"
6 (6½, 6¾)"

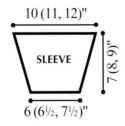

10 (11, 12)"
SLEEVE
7 (8, 9)"
6 (6½, 7½)"

g o l d e n   c h i l d

SIZE

One size fits 6-18 months.

FINISHED MEASUREMENTS

• Circumference 16½"/42cm

MATERIALS

• 1 1¾oz/50g ball (approx 120yd/110m) of Berroco, Inc. Suede (nylon) in #3714 Hopalong Cassidy (MC) (4)
• 1 1¾oz/50g ball (approx 90yd/83m) of Berroco, Inc. Plush (nylon) in #1901 crema (CC) (5)
• Size H/8 (5mm) crochet hook or size to obtain gauge
• Yarn needle

GAUGE

12 sts and 12 rnds to 4"/10cm over hdc using size H/8 (5mm) hook and MC. Take time to check gauge.

NOTE

It's sometimes difficult seeing the sts when working with furry yarn. For best results, count sts as you work across each row to make sure you do not skip or miss a st.

HAT

With MC, ch 50. Taking care not to twist ch, join ch with a sl st forming a ring. **Rnd 1 (RS)** Hdc in same ch as joining, then hdc in each ch around—50 sts. Join rnd with a sl st in first st. Ch 2, turn (back seam). **Rnd 2** Hdc in each st around. Join rnd with a sl st in first st. Ch 2, turn. Rep rnd 2 until 9 rnds have been completed. **Next rnd** Working in back lps only, hdc in each st around. Join rnd with a sl st in first st. Ch 2, turn.

Crown shaping

Dec rnd 1 *Hdc in next 3 sts, dec 1 st over next 2 sts; rep from * around—40 sts. Join rnd with a sl st in first st. Ch 2, turn. **Dec rnd 2** Rep last rnd—32 sts. Join rnd with a sl st in first st. Ch 2, turn. **Dec rnd 3** *Hdc in next 2 sts, dec 1 st over next 2 sts; rep from * around—24 sts. Join rnd with a sl st in first st. Ch 2, turn. **Dec rnd 4** Rep last rnd—18 sts. Join rnd with a sl st in first st. Ch 2, turn. **Dec rnd 5** *Hdc in next st, dec 1 st over next 2 sts; rep from * around—12 sts. Join rnd with a sl st in first st. Ch 2, turn. **Dec rnd 6** [Dec 1 st over next 2 sts] 6 times—6 sts. Fasten off leaving a long tail. Thread tail into yarn needle and weave through sts. Pull tight to gather, fasten off securely.

Back flap

With bottom edge of hat at top, count 5 sts to the right of back seam. Join MC with a hdc in bottom lp of beg ch, cont working in bottom lps, hdc in next 10 lps. Ch 2, turn—11 sts. Working in hdc, work even for 3 more rows. Fasten off.

Right ear flap

From RS, count 1 st to the left of back flap. Join MC with a hdc in bottom lp of beg ch, hdc in next 11 lps. Ch 2, turn—12 sts. **Row 1** Dec 1 st over first 2 sts, hdc in next 8 sts, dec 1 st over last 2 sts—10 sts. Ch 2, turn. **Row 2** Hdc in each st across. Ch 2, turn. **Row 3** Dec 1 st over first 2 sts, hdc in next 6 sts, dec 1 st over last 2 sts—8 sts. Ch 2, turn. **Row 4** Hdc in each st across. Ch 2, turn. **Row 5** Dec 1 st over first 2 sts, hdc in next 4 sts, dec 1 st over last 2 sts— 6 sts. Ch 2, turn. **Row 6** Dec 1 st over first 2 sts, hdc in next 2 sts, dec 1 st over last 2 sts—4 sts. Ch 2, turn. **Row 7** [Dec 1 st over next 2 sts] twice—2 sts. Fasten off.

Left ear flap

From RS, count 13 sts to the right of back flap. Join MC with a hdc in bottom lp of beg ch, hdc in next 11 lps. Ch 2, turn—12 sts. Cont to work as for right ear flap.

Bill

From RS, count 1 st to the left of right ear flap. Join CC with a hdc in bottom lp of beg ch, hdc in next 10 lps. Ch 2, turn—11 sts. **Row 2** Hdc in each st across. Ch 2, turn. **Row 3** Dec 1 st over first 2 sts, hdc in next 7 sts, dec 1 st over last 2 sts—9 sts. Ch 2, turn. **Row 4** Dec 1 st over first 2 sts, hdc in next 5 sts, dec 1 st over last 2 sts— 7 sts. Ch 2, turn. **Row 5** Dec 1 st over first 2 sts, hdc in next 3 sts, dec 1 st over last 2 sts—5 sts. Fasten off.

FINISHING

Hat edging

From RS, join CC with a hdc in next st from left edge of bill. Making sure that work lies flat, hdc evenly around entire edge to next st from right edge of bill. Fasten off.

Bill edging

From WS, join MC with a hdc in RH edge of row 2. Making sure that work lies flat, hdc up right edge, across top edge and down left edge to LH edge of row 2. Fasten off. Fold up bill to RS and tack in place.

Ties

(make 2)

With CC, ch 23. **Row 1** Hdc in 3rd ch from hook and in each ch across—21 sts. Fasten off. Sew ties to ear flaps; as shown.

f e e t   f i r s t

SIZES

Instructions are written for size 6-12 months. Changes for size 12-18 months are in parentheses.

MATERIALS

• 1 1¾oz/50g balls (each approx 120yd/110m) of Berroco, Inc. Suede (nylon) each in #3717 Wild Bill Hickcock (A) and #3714 Hopalong Cassidy (B) (4)
• 1 1¾oz/50g ball (approx 90yd/83m) of Berroco, Inc. Plush (nylon) in #1901 crema (C) (5)
• For size 6-12 months, size G/6 (4mm) crochet hook or size to obtain gauge
• For size 12-18 months, size H/8 (5mm) crochet hook or size to obtain gauge
• One small safety pin
• Yarn needle

GAUGES

• 16 sts and 19 rows to 4"/10cm over sc using size G/6 (4mm) hook and A.
• 14 sts and 17 rows to 4"/10cm over sc using size H/8 (5mm) hook and A.
Take time to check gauges.

BOOTIE

Beg at center bottom of sole, with size G/4mm (H/8mm) hook and A, ch 14. **Rnd 1** Sc in 2nd ch from hook, sc in next 9 ch, hdc in next ch, work 2 hdc in next ch, 3 hdc in last ch. Turn to bottom lps of beg ch. Work 2 hdc in each of first 2 lps, hdc in next lp, sc in next 9 lps, work 2 sc in last lp—32 sts. Mark last st made with the safety pin. You will be working in a spiral (to rnd 12) marking the last st made with the safety pin to indicate end of rnd.
Rnd 2 Work 2 sc in next st, sc in next 12 sts, [work 2 sc in next st, sc in next st] 3 times, sc in next 11 sts, 2 sc in next st, sc in next st—37 sts.
Rnd 3 Work 2 sc in next st, sc in next 13 sts, [work 2 sc in next st, sc in next st] twice, [sc in next st, 2 sc in next st] twice, sc in next 13 sts, work 2 sc in next st, sc in next st—43 sts.
Rnd 4 Working in back lps only, sc in each st around. Change to B.
Rnd 5 Sc in each st around.
Rnd 6 Sc in next 16 sts, [dec 1 st over next 2 sts, sc in next st] 4 times, sc in next 15 sts—39 sts.

Rnd 7 Sc in next 15 sts, [dec 1 st over next 2 sts] 5 times, sc in next 14 sts—34 sts.

Rnd 8 Sc in next 14 sts, hdc in next 2 sts, working in hdc, dec 1 st over next 2 sts, hdc in next 2 sts, sc in next 14 sts—33 sts.

Rnd 9 Sc in next 14 sts, hdc in next 2 sts, working in hdc, dec 1 st over next 2 sts, hdc in next 2 sts, sc in next 14 sts—32 sts.

Rnd 10 Sc in next 13 sts, [working in hdc, dec 1 st over next 2 sts] 3 times, sc in next 13 sts—29 sts.

Rnd 11 Working in sc, sc in next 10 sts, [dec 1 st over next 2 sts] twice, sc in next st, [dec 1 st over next 2 sts] twice, sc next 10 sts—25 sts. Drop safety pin. Join rnd with a sl st in next st. Ch 2, turn.

Rnds 12, 13, 14 and 15 Hdc in each st around. Join rnd with a sl st in first st. Ch 2, turn. After rnd 15 is completed, change to C, ch 2, turn.

Rnd 16 Hdc in each st around. Join rnd with a sl st in first st. Fasten off.

FINISHING

Embroidery

Use one strand of CC in needle throughout and refer to photo. For vertical stitching lines on each side of bootie, measure 1"/2.5cm from center front. Working from rnd 15, sew running stitches (going over one rnd and under next rnd) to rnd 5. For horizontal stitching line across instep, beg at one vertical stitching line at rnd 8. Sew running stitches (going over one st and under next st) to opposite side.

f u r   e v e r

SIZES

Instructions are written for size 6 months. Changes for sizes 12 months and 18 months are in parentheses.

FINISHED MEASUREMENTS

• Chest (buttoned) 22 (24, 26)"/56 (61, 66)cm
• Length 11 (12, 13)"/28 (30.5, 33)cm
• Upper arm 10 (11, 12)"/25.5 (28, 30.5)cm

MATERIALS

• 4 (4, 5) 1³/₄oz/50g balls (each approx 60yd/54m) of Lion Brand Yarn Co. Fun Fur (polyester) in #206 confetti ⑤
• Size I/9 (5.5mm) crochet hook or size to obtain gauge
• Three ³/₄"/19mm buttons

GAUGE

11 sts and 10 rows to 4"/10cm over sc using size I/9 (5.5mm) hook.
Take time to check gauge.

NOTE

It's sometimes difficult seeing the sts when working with furry yarn. For best results, count sts as you work across each row to make sure you do not skip or miss a st.

BACK

Ch 31 (35, 37). **Row 1** Sc in 2nd ch from hook and in each ch across—30 (34, 36) sts. Ch 1, turn. **Row 2** Sc in each st across. Ch 1, turn. Rep row 2 for pat st and work even until piece measures 11 (12, 13)"/26.5 (28, 30.5, 33)cm from beg. Fasten off.

LEFT FRONT

Ch 17 (19, 20). **Row 1** Sc in 2nd ch from hook and in each ch across—16 (18, 19) sts. Ch 1, turn. Work even in sc until piece measures 7 (7¹/₂, 8)"/17.5 (19, 20.5)cm from beg.
Neck shaping
Next row Dec 1 st at beg of row, then at same edge 4 (5, 5) times more—11 (12, 13) sts. Work even until same length as back. Fasten off.

RIGHT FRONT

Work as for left front reversing neck shaping.

SLEEVES

Ch 17 (19, 21). **Row 1** Sc in 2nd ch from hook and in each ch across—16 (18, 20) sts. Ch 1, turn. Work in sc and inc 1 st each side on next row, then every other row 5 times more—28 (30, 32) sts. Work even until piece measures 7 (8, 9)"/17.5 (20.5, 23)cm from beg. Fasten off.

FINISHING

Sew shoulder seams. Place markers 5 (5½, 6)"/12.5 (14, 15)cm down from shoulder seams on fronts and back. Sew sleeves to armholes between markers. Sew side and sleeve seams.

Button loops

(make 3)

Ch 8. Fasten off leaving a long tail for sewing. Fold ch in half to make loop. On right front, sew first loop at beg of neck shaping and the rest spaced 2"/5cm apart. Sew on buttons.

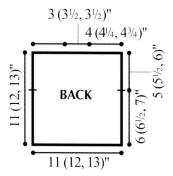

3 (3½, 3½)"
4 (4¼, 4¾)"
11 (12, 13)"
BACK
5 (5½, 6)"
6 (6½, 7)"
11 (12, 13)"

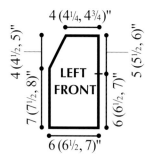

4 (4¼, 4¾)"
4 (4½, 5)"
7 (7½, 8)"
LEFT FRONT
5 (5½, 6)"
6 (6½, 7)"
6 (6½, 7)"

10 (11, 12)"
SLEEVE
7 (8, 9)"
6 (6½, 7)"

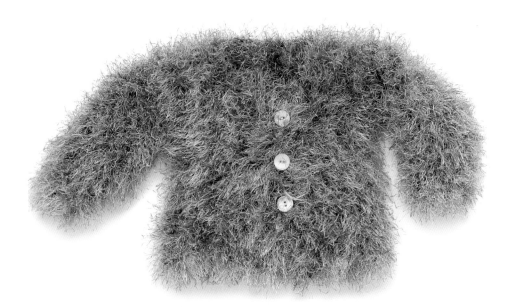

poncho power

SIZE

Instructions are written for size 12-18 months.

FINISHED MEASUREMENTS

• Width 22"/56cm
• Length 12"/30.5cm (not including fringe)

MATERIALS

• 2 1¾oz /50g balls (each approx 103yd/95m) of Tahki Yarns/Tahki•Stacy Charles, Inc. New Tweed (wool/silk/cotton/viscose) each in #025 medium brown (A) and #05 dark brown (B) (4)
• 1 ball each in #1 beige (C) and #024 light brown (D)
• Size H/8 (5mm) crochet hook or size to obtain gauge
• 1yd/1m of leather cord (optional)

GAUGE

12 sts and 10 rows to 4"/10cm over hdc using size H/8 (5mm) hook.
Take time to check gauge.

NOTES

1) See instructions on page 130 for working color changes for rows.
2) See instructions on page 130 for working color changes for charts.

BACK

With A, ch 68. **Row 1 (WS)** Hdc in 3rd ch from hook and in each ch across—66 sts. Ch 2, turn. **Row 2** Hdc in each st across. Ch 2, turn. Rep row 2 for pat st and work even for one more row.

Chart 1

Row 1 (RS) Beg with st 1 and work to st 6, then rep sts 1-6 10 times more. Cont to foll chart in this way to row 4, end with a WS row.

Chart 2

Row 1 (RS) Beg with st 1 and work to st 11, then rep sts 1-11 5 times more. Cont to foll chart in this way to row 21, end with a RS row.

Chart 3

Row 1 (WS) Beg with st 6 and work to st 1, then rep sts 6-1 10 times more. Cont to foll chart in this way to row 5; piece should measure 12"/30.5cm from beg. Fasten off.

FRONT

Work as for back until row 18 of chart 2 has been completed, end with a WS row; piece should measure 9"/23cm from beg.

Left neck shaping

Row 19 (RS) Work across first 33 sts. Ch 2, turn. Dec 1 st at beg of next row, then at same edge every row 5 times. AT SAME TIME, when chart 2 has been completed, work chart 3. Work even on 28 sts to row 5 of chart 3. Fasten off.

Right neck shaping

Row 19 (RS) Join A with a sc in next st, work to end. Ch 2, turn. Cont to work as for left neck, reversing shaping.

FINISHING

Sew shoulder seams.

Neck edging

From RS, join A with a sc in right shoulder seam. **Rnd 1** Making sure that work lies flat, sc evenly around neck edge. Join rnd with a sl st in first st. Fasten off.

Fringe

For each fringe, cut 4 strands of B 9"/23cm long. Use hook to pull through and knot fringe. Knot 17 fringes across front and back bottom edges. Weave optional leather cord around neck edge, beg and ending at center front. Tie cord at neck, then knot ends.

Color Key

- ■ Medium Brown (A)
- ■ Dark Brown (B)
- ☐ Beige (C)
- ▨ Light Brown (D)

Chart 1

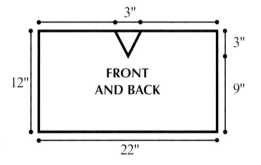

Chart 2

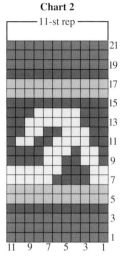

Chart 3

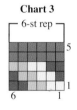

FRONT AND BACK — 3" (top), 3" and 9" (right side), 12" (left side), 22" (bottom)

w r a p   s t a r

SIZES

Instructions are written for size 6 months. Changes for sizes 12 months and 18 months are in parentheses.

FINISHED MEASUREMENTS

• Chest (buttoned) 20 (22, 23$\frac{1}{2}$)"/51 (56, 59.5)cm
• Length 8$\frac{1}{2}$ (9$\frac{1}{2}$, 10)"/21.5 (24, 25.5)cm
• Upper arm 9 (10, 11)"/23 (25.5, 28)cm

MATERIALS

• 2 (2, 3) 1$\frac{3}{4}$oz/50g balls (each approx 136yd/125m) of Debbie Bliss/KFI Cashmerino Baby (wool/microfiber/cashmere) in #600 pink ③
• Size F/5 (3.75mm) crochet hook or size to obtain gauge
• Three $\frac{1}{2}$"/13mm buttons
• Two medium snaps
• Matching sewing thread
• Sewing needle

GAUGES

• 17 sts and 13 rows to 4"/10cm over hdc using size F/5 (3.75mm) hook.
• 17 sts and 18 rows to 4"/10cm over pat st using size F/5 (3.75mm) hook.
Take time to check gauges.

PATTERN STITCH

Rows 1-4 Sc in each st across. Ch 1, turn. After row 4 is completed, ch 3, turn.
Row 5 Dc in first st, *sk next st, dc in next st, dc in sk st; rep from *, end dc in last st. Ch 1, turn.
Rep rows 1-5 for pat st.

BACK

Ch 44 (48, 52). **Row 1 (WS)** Hdc in 3rd ch from hook and in each ch across—42 (46, 50) sts. Ch 2, turn. **Row 2** Hdc in each st across. Ch 2, turn. Rep row 2 and work even until piece measures 4$\frac{1}{2}$ (5, 5)"/11.5 (12.5, 12.5)cm from beg, end with a WS row. Fasten off. Turn work.

Armhole shaping

Next row (RS) Sk first 4 sts, join yarn with a hdc in next st, work across to within last 4 sts. Ch 2, turn—34 (38, 42) sts. Work even until armhole measures 4 (4$\frac{1}{2}$, 5)"/10 (11.5, 12.5)cm. Fasten off.

LEFT FRONT

Ch 43 (47, 51). **Foundation row (WS)** Sc in 2nd ch from hook and in each ch across—42 (46, 50) sts. Ch 1, turn. Cont in pat st and work even until 8 rows have been completed, end with a WS row.

Neck shaping

Next row (RS) Dec 1 st at end of row, then at same edge every row 27 (29, 31) times more. AT THE SAME TIME, when piece measures 4$\frac{1}{2}$ (5, 5)"/11.5 (12.5, 12.5)cm from beg, end with a WS row. Fasten off. Turn work.

Armhole shaping

Next row (RS) Sk first 4 sts, keeping to pat st join yarn with either a sc or dc, work to end. When all neck dec have been completed, work even on 10 (12, 14) sts until piece measures same length as back. Fasten off.

RIGHT FRONT

Ch 43 (47, 51). **Foundation row (WS)** Sc in 2nd ch from hook and in each ch across—42 (46, 50) sts. Ch 1, turn. Cont in pat st and work buttonholes as foll: **Row 1** Sc in first st, ch 1, sk next st, sc in each st to end. Ch 1, turn. **Row 2** Sc in each st across, working one sc in ch-1 sp. Ch 1, turn. **Row 3** Sc in each st across. Ch 1, turn. **Row 4 (WS)** Sc in each st to within last 2 sts, ch 1, sk next st, sc in last st. Ch 3, turn. **Row 5** Dc in first st, sk next ch-1 sp, dc in next st, dc in ch-1 sp, *sk next st, dc in next st, dc in sk st; rep from *, end dc in last st. Ch 1, turn. **Row 6 (WS)** Rep row 4. **Row 7** Rep row 2. Ch 1, turn. **Row 8** Sc in each st across. Ch 1, turn. Cont to work as for left front, reversing shaping.

SLEEVES

Ch 28 (30, 32). **Row 1 (WS)** Hdc in 3rd ch from hook and in each ch across—26 (28, 30) sts. Ch 2, turn. Work in hdc and inc 1 st each side on next row, then every 4th row 5 (6, 7) times more—38 (42, 46) sts.

Work even until piece measures 8 (9, 10)"/20.5 (23, 25.5)cm from beg. Fasten off.

FINISHING

Sew shoulder seams.

Picot edging

From RS, join yarn with a sc in beg of right neck shaping. **Row 1** Making sure that work lies flat, sc evenly along entire neck edge to beg of left neck shaping. Ch 1, turn. **Row 2** Sc in each st across. Ch 1, turn. **Row 3 (RS)** Sc in first 2 sts, *ch 3, sl st in 3rd ch from hook, sc in next 3 sts; rep from * to end. Fasten off. Set in sleeves. Sew side and sleeve seams. Sew on buttons. On RS of left front, sew one half of first snap set ¹⁄₂"/1.3cm from bottom edge and the 2nd snap at beg of neck shaping. On WS, sew other side of snap sets to left side seam.

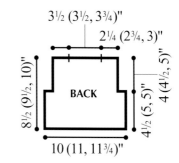

BACK

3½ (3½, 3¾)"
2¼ (2¾, 3)"
8½ (9½, 10)"
4½ (5, 5)"
4 (4½, 5)"
10 (11, 11¾)"

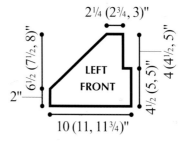

LEFT FRONT

2¼ (2¾, 3)"
6½ (7½, 8)"
2"
4½ (5, 5)"
4 (4½, 5)"
10 (11, 11¾)"

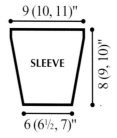

SLEEVE

9 (10, 11)"
8 (9, 10)"
6 (6½, 7)"

SIZES

Instructions are written for size 6 months. Changes for sizes 12 months and 18 months are in parentheses.

FINISHED MEASUREMENTS

Pullover
- Chest 21 (23, 25)"/53.5 (58.5, 63.5)cm
- Length 11 (11½, 12)"/28 (29, 30.5)cm
- Upper arm 9 (9½, 10)"/23 (24, 25.5)cm

Pants
- Waist 21 (24, 26)"/53.5 (61, 66)cm
- Length 15 (16½, 18)"/38 (42, 45.5)cm

MATERIALS

Pullover
- 4 (5, 5) 1¾oz/50g balls (each approx 136yd/125m) of Debbie Bliss/KFI Cashmerino Baby (wool/microfiber/cashmere) in #503 olive (A) **3**

Pants
- 3 (4, 4) balls in #203 teal (B)
- Size G/6 (4mm) crochet hook or size to obtain gauge
- Three ½"/13mm buttons
- ¾yd/.75m of ½"/13mm-wide elastic
- White sewing thread
- Sewing needle

GAUGES

- 20 sts and 17 rows to 4"/10cm over cable pat using size G/6 (4mm) hook.
- 16 sts and 16 rows to 4"/10cm over pat st using size G/6 (4mm) hook.

Take time to check gauges.

STITCH GLOSSARY

FPDC (Front Post Double Crochet)
Yo, working from front to back to front, insert hook around post of st of row below, yo and draw up a lp, [yo and draw through 2 lps on hook] twice.

BPDC (Back Post Double Crochet)
Yo, working from back to front to back, insert hook around post of st of row below, yo and draw up a lp, [yo and draw through 2 lps on hook] twice.

PATTERN STITCH

Row 1 *Sc in front lp of next st, sc in back lp of next st; rep from * to end. Ch 1, turn. Rep row 1 for pat st.

CABLE TWIST

(Worked over 3 sts)

Row 1 (RS) Sk 2 sts, FPDC around next st, ch 1, FPDC around first sk st (leave 2nd st unworked).

Row 2 BPDC, sc in ch-1 sp, BPDC. Rep rows 1 and 2 for cable twist.

PULLOVER

FRONT

With A, ch 54 (58, 62). **Foundation row 1 (RS)** Sc in 2nd ch from hook and in each ch across—53 (57, 61) sts. Ch 1, turn.

Foundation row 2 Work row 1 of pat st. Ch 1, turn.

Beg pat sts

Row 1 (RS) Work pat st across first 5 (7, 9) sts, [work row 1 of cable twist over next 3 sts, work pat st across next 7 sts] 4 times, work row 1 of cable twist over next 3 sts, work pat st across last 5 (7, 9) sts. Ch 1, turn.

Row 2 Work pat st across first 5 (7, 9) sts, [work row 2 of cable twist over next 3 sts, work pat st across next 7 sts] 4 times, work row 2 of cable twist over next 3 sts, work pat st across last 5 (7, 9) sts. Ch 1, turn.

Row 3 Sc across first 5 (7, 9) sts, [work row 1 of cable twist over next 3 sts, sc across next 7 sts] 4 times, work row 1 of cable twist over next 3 sts, sc across last 5 (7, 9) sts. Ch 1, turn.

Row 4 Sc across first 5 (7, 9) sts, [work row 2 of cable twist over next 3 sts, sc across

next 7 sts] 4 times, work row 2 of cable twist over next 3 sts, sc across last 5 (7, 9) sts. Ch 1, turn. Rep rows 1-4 until piece measures 7 (7$\frac{1}{2}$, 8)"/17.5 (19, 20.5)cm from beg, end with a WS row. Mark beg and end of last row for beg of neck opening.

LEFT FRONT

Next row (RS) Work across first 25 (27, 29) sts. Ch 1, turn. Work even until opening measures 2$\frac{1}{2}$"/6.5cm, end with a WS row.

Left neck shaping

Next row (RS) Work across first 21 (23, 25) sts. Ch 1, turn. Dec 1 st at beg of next row, then at same edge every row 5 times more—15 (17, 19) sts. Work even until piece measures 11 (11$\frac{1}{2}$, 12)"/28 (29, 30.5)cm from beg. Fasten off.

RIGHT FRONT

Next row (RS) Sk next 3 sts, join A with a sc in next st, work to end. Ch 1, turn—25 (27, 29) sts. Cont to work as for left front, reversing neck shaping.

BACK

With A, ch 54 (58, 62). **Foundation row 1 (RS)** Sc in 2nd ch from hook and in each

ch across—53 (57, 61) sts. Ch 1, turn.
Foundation row 2 Work row 1 of pat st across. Ch 1, turn.
Beg pat sts
Rows 1 and 2 Work in pat st. Ch 1, turn.
Rows 3 and 4 Sc in each st across. Ch 1, turn. Rep rows 1-4 until piece measures same length as front. Fasten off.

SLEEVES

With A, ch 32 (34, 36). **Foundation row 1 (RS)** Sc in 2nd ch from hook and in each ch across—31 (33, 35) sts. Ch 1, turn.
Foundation row 2 Work row 1 of pat st across. Ch 1, turn.
Beg pat sts
Row 1 (RS) Work pat st across first 14 (15, 16) sts, work row 1 of cable twist over next 3 sts, work pat st across last 14 (15, 16) sts. Ch 1, turn.
Row 2 Work pat st across first 14 (15, 16) sts, work row 2 of cable twist over next 3 sts, work pat st across last 14 (15, 16) sts. Ch 1, turn.
Row 3 Sc across first 14 (15, 16) sts, work row 1 of cable twist over next 3 sts, sc across last 14 (15, 16) sts. Ch 1, turn.

Row 4 Sc across first 14 (15, 16) sts, work row 2 of cable twist over next 3 sts, sc across last 14 (15, 16) sts. Ch 1, turn. Rep rows 1-4 for pat sts. AT SAME TIME, working new sts into pat sts, inc 1 st each side every 4th row 7 times—45 (47, 49) sts. Work even until piece measures 7 (7, 8)"/17.5 (17.5, 20.5)cm from beg. Fasten off.

FINISHING

Sew shoulder seams.
Front and neck bands
With RS of right front facing, join A with a sc above neck opening. **Row 1** Making sure that work lies flat, sc evenly up right front edge, around neck edge, then down left front edge, working 3 sc in each corner st. Ch 1, turn. Place markers on right front for boy (or left front for girl) for 3 buttons, with the first 1 st from neck edge, the 2nd 2 sts from top of neck opening and the 3rd spaced evenly between. **Row 2 (buttonhole row)** *Sc in each st to marker, ch 1, sk next st; rep from * 3 times, then cont in sc to end, working 3 sc in each corner st. Ch 1, turn.
Row 3 Sc in each st across, working a sc

in each ch-1 sp and working 3 sc in each corner st. Fasten off. Lap buttonhole band over button band and sew bottom edges of bands in place. Place markers 4½ (4¾, 5)"/11.5 (12, 12.5)cm down from shoulder seams on front and back. Sew sleeves to armholes between markers. Sew side and sleeve seams. Sew on buttons.

Bottom edging

From RS, join A with a sl st in right side seam. **Rnd 1** Ch 1, making sure that work lies flat, sc evenly around edge. Join rnd with a sl st in first st. **Rnds 2 and 3** Ch 1, sc in each around. Join rnd with a sl st in first st. Fasten off.

Sleeve edging

From RS, join A with a sl st in underarm seam. Cont to work as for bottom edging.

PANTS

LEFT LEG

With B, ch 31 (33, 37). **Foundation row (RS)** Sc in 2nd ch from hook and in each ch across—30 (32, 36) sts. Ch 1, turn. Cont in pat st and inc 1 st each side on next row, then every other row 11 (13, 13)

times more—54 (60, 64) sts. Work even until piece measures 7 (8, 9)"/17.5 (20.5, 23)cm from beg. Fasten off. Turn work.

Crotch shaping

Next row Sk first 2 sts, join B with a sc in next st, work across to within last 2 sts. Ch 1, turn—50 (56, 60) sts. Dec 1 st each side every row 4 times—42 (48, 52) sts. Work even until piece measures 15 (16½, 18)"/38 (42, 45.5)cm from beg. Fasten off.

RIGHT LEG

Work as for left leg.

FINISHING

Sew front, back and leg seams. Measure waist and add 1"/2.5cm. Cut elastic to measurement. For casing for elastic, fold top edge ¾"/2cm to WS and sew in place leaving a 1"/2.5cm opening at center back. Insert elastic through casing. Sew ends of elastic tog. Sew opening closed.

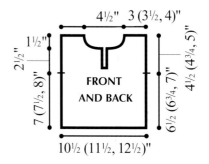

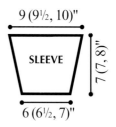

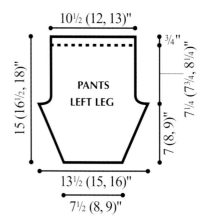

summer love

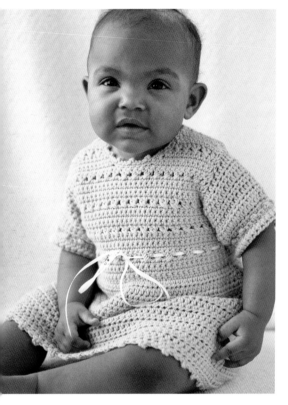

SIZES

Instructions are written for size 6 months. Changes for sizes 12 months and 18 months are in parentheses.

FINISHED MEASUREMENTS

• Chest 18 (20, 22)"/45.5 (51, 56)cm
• Length 14 (16, 18)"/35.5 (40.5, 45.5)cm
• Upper arm 8 (9, 10)"/20.5 (23, 25.5)cm

MATERIALS

• 3 (4, 5) 1 ³/₄oz/50g balls (each approx 136yd/125m) of Debbie Bliss/KFI Cashmerino Baby (wool/microfiber/ cashmere) in #600 pink ③
• Size F/5 (3.75mm) crochet hook or size to obtain gauge
• Three ¹/₂"/13mm buttons
• 1 ¹/₄yd/1.25m of ³/₁₆"/5mm-wide ivory satin ribbon

GAUGES

• 17 sts and 13 rows to 4"/10cm over hdc using size F/5 (3.75mm) hook.
• 17 sts and 18 rows to 4"/10cm over pat st using size F/5 (3.75mm) hook.
Take time to check gauges.

NOTES

1) Back and front bodices are made separately, then sewn tog.
2) Skirt is made in one piece from bodice to hem.

PATTERN STITCH

Rows 1-4 Sc in each st across. Ch 1, turn. After row 4 is completed, ch 3, turn.

Row 5 Dc in first st, *sk next st, dc in next st, dc in sk st; rep from *, end dc in last st. Ch 1, turn.
Rep rows 1-5 for pat st.

BACK BODICE

Ch 40 (44, 48). **Row 1 (WS)** Hdc in 3rd ch from hook and in each ch across—38 (42, 46) sts. Ch 2, turn. **Row 2** Hdc in each st across. Ch 2, turn. Rep row 2 and work even until piece measures 3 (3¹/₂, 4)"/7.5 (9, 10)cm from beg, end with a WS row. Fasten off. Turn work.

Armhole shaping

Next row (RS) Sk first 4 sts, join yarn with a hdc in next st, work across to within last 4 sts. Ch 2, turn—30 (34, 38) sts. Work even until armhole measures 4 (4¹/₂, 5)"/10 (11.5, 12.5)cm. Fasten off.

FRONT BODICE

Ch 39 (43, 47). **Row 1** Sc in 2nd ch from hook and in each ch across—38 (42, 46) sts. Ch 1, turn. Beg with row 2, cont in pat st and work even until piece measures 3 (3¹/₂, 4)"/7.5 (9, 10)cm from beg, end with row 1, 2 or 5. Fasten off. Turn work.

Armhole shaping

Next row (RS) Sk first 4 sts, join yarn with a sc in next st, work across to within last 4 sts. Keeping to pat st, ch 1 or 3, turn—30 (34, 38) sts. Work even until armhole measures 2 (2¹/₂, 3)"/5 (6.5, 7.5)cm.

Left neck shaping

Next row (RS) Work across first 12 (13, 15) sts, ch 1 or 3, turn. Dec 1 st from neck edge every row 3 (3, 4) times—9 (10, 11) sts. Work even until piece measures same length as back. Fasten off.

Right neck shaping

Next row (RS) Sk 6 (8, 8) center sts, join yarn with a sc or dc in next st, work to end. Cont to work as for left neck, reversing shaping. Ch 1, turn. **Buttonhole band** Sc in first 1 (2, 1) sts, [ch 1, sk next st, sc in next 2 (2, 3) sts] twice, ch 1, sk next st, sc in last st. **Next row** Sc in each st across, working 1 sc in each ch-1 sp. Fasten off. Sew side seams.

SKIRT

From RS, join yarn with a sl st in right side seam. **Rnd 1** Ch 1, working through bottom lps of row 1, sc in each st around—76 (84, 92) sts. Join rnd with a sl st in first st; turn. **Rnd 2** Ch 2, *work 2 hdc in next st, hdc in next st; rep from * around—114 (126, 138) sts. Join rnd with a sl st in first st; turn. **Rnd 3** Ch 2, hdc in each st around. Join rnd with a sl st in first st; turn. Rep rnd 3 and work even until skirt measures 7 (8, 9)"/17.5 (20.5, 23)cm from beg, end with a WS row. **Picot row** Sc in first 2 sts, *ch 3, sl st in 3rd ch from hook, sc in next 3 sts; rep from * around. Join rnd with a sl st in first st. Fasten off.

SLEEVES

Ch 32 (34, 36). **Row 1 (WS)** Hdc in 3rd ch from hook and in each ch across—30 (32, 34) sts. Ch 2, turn. Work in hdc and inc 1 st each side on next row, then every 3rd row 1 (2, 3) times more—34 (38, 42) sts. Work even until piece measures 4 (4½, 5)"/10 (11.5, 12.5)cm from beg. Fasten off.

FINISHING

Sew left shoulder seam.

Neck edging

With RS of right back shoulder facing, sk first 9 (10, 11) shoulder sts, join yarn with a sc in next st. Making sure that work lies flat, work picot row around neck edge as foll: Sc in next st, *ch 3, sl st in 3rd ch from hook, sc in next 3 sts; rep from * to right front shoulder. Fasten off. Sew on buttons. Fasten buttons into buttonholes, then pin right shoulder to secure overlap. Sew sleeve seams. Set in sleeves.

Sleeve edging

From RS, join yarn with a sl st in underarm seam. **Row 1** Ch 1, working in bottom lps of row 1, sc in first 2 lps, *ch 3, sl st in 3rd ch from hook, sc in next 3 lps; rep from * around. Join rnd with a sl st in first sc. Fasten off. Weave ribbon through first row 5 of pat st on bodice, beg and ending at center front. Tie ribbon in a bow and trim ends at an angle.

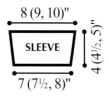

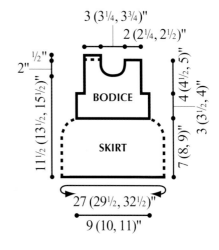

3 (3¼, 3¾)"

2 (2¼, 2½)"

½"

2"

11½ (13½, 15½)"

BODICE

SKIRT

4 (4½, 5)"

3 (3½, 4)"

7 (8, 9)"

27 (29½, 32½)"

9 (10, 11)"

8 (9, 10)"

SLEEVE

4 (4½, 5)"

7 (7½, 8)"

a h o y ,   m a t e y !

SIZES

Instructions are written for size 6 months. Changes for sizes 12 months and 18 months are in parentheses.

FINISHED MEASUREMENTS

Top

• Chest 20 (22, 24)"/51 (56, 61)cm

• Length 10½ (11½, 12½)"/26.5 (29, 31.5)cm

• Upper arm 8 (9, 10)"/20.5 (23, 25.5)cm

Shorts

• Waist 21 (24, 26)"/53.5 (61, 66)cm

• Length 11 (12, 12½)"/28 (30.5, 31.5)cm

MATERIALS

Top

• 2 (3, 3) 1¾oz/50g balls (each approx 136yd/125m) of Patons Grace (cotton) in #60005 snow (A) **2**

• 1 ball each in #60705 cardinal (B) and #60134 royal (C)

Shorts

• 3 (3, 4) balls in #60134 royal (C)

• Size F/5 (3.75mm) crochet hook or size to obtain gauge

• Two ⅞"/22mm red star buttons

• ¾yd/.75m of ½"/13mm-wide elastic

• White sewing thread

• Sewing needle

GAUGE

20 sts and 17 rows to 4"/10cm over hdc using size F/5 (3.75mm) hook.
Take time to check gauge.

NOTE

See page 130 for working color changes for rows.

STRIPE PATTERN

Work 4 rows A in hdc and 2 rows B in sc. Rep these 6 rows for stripe pat.

TOP

BACK

With A, ch 52 (58, 62). **Row 1 (WS)** Hdc in 3rd ch from hook and in each ch across—50 (56, 60) sts. Ch 2, turn. **Rows 2-4** Hdc in each st across. Ch 2, turn. **Row 5** Rep row 2. Join B, ch 1, turn. **Rows 6 and 7** Sc in each st across. Ch 1, turn. When row 7 is completed, join A, ch 2, turn. Cont in stripe pat and work even until 4th B stripe has been completed. Cont with A and hdc until piece measures 6½ (7, 7½)"/16.5 (17.5, 19)cm from beg, end with a WS row. Fasten off. Turn work.

Armhole shaping

Next row Sk first 5 sts, join A with a hdc in next st, work across to within last 5 sts. Ch 2, turn—40 (46, 50) sts. Work even until armhole measures 4 (4$^{1}/_{2}$, 5)"/10 (11.5, 12.5)cm. Fasten off.

FRONT

Work as for back until armhole measures 2 (2$^{1}/_{2}$, 3)"/5 (6.5, 7.5)cm, end with a WS row.

Left neck shaping

Next row (RS) Work across first 17 (19, 20) sts, ch 2, turn. Dec 1 st from neck edge every row 5 times—12 (14, 15) sts. Work even until armhole measures 4 (4$^{1}/_{2}$, 5)"/10 (11.5, 12.5)cm, end with a WS row. Ch 1, turn.

Buttonhole band

Next (buttonhole) row (RS) Sc in first 3 (4, 4) sts, ch 2, sk next 2 sts, sc in next 4 (5, 6) sts, ch 2, sk next 2 sts, sc in last st. Ch 1, turn. **Next row** Sc across, working 2 sc in each ch-2 sp. Fasten off.

Right neck shaping

Next row (RS) Sk 6 (8, 10) center sts, join A with a hdc in next st, work to end. Cont to work as for left neck, reversing shaping, until armhole measures 4 (4$\frac{1}{2}$, 5)"/10 (11.5, 12.5)cm, end with a WS row. Fasten off.

SLEEVES

With A, ch 36 (38, 40). **Row 1 (WS)** Hdc in 3rd ch from hook and in each ch across—34 (36, 38) sts. Ch 2, turn. Work in hdc and inc 1 st each side on next row, then every 3rd row 2 (3, 5) times more—40 (44, 50) sts. Work even until piece measures 4 (4$\frac{1}{2}$, 5)"/10 (11.5, 12.5)cm from beg. Fasten off.

FINISHING

Sew right shoulder seam.

Button band

With RS of back facing, sk first 28 (32, 35) sts, join A with a sc in next, then sc in last 12 (14, 15) sts. Ch 1, turn. Cont to work in sc for one more row. Fasten off.

Neck edging

From RS, join C with a sl st in side edge of left front buttonhole band. Making sure that work lies flat, sc evenly along entire neck edge. Ch 1, turn. **Next row** Sc in each st across. Fasten off. Sew on buttons. Fasten buttons into buttonholes, then pin left shoulder to secure overlap. Set in sleeves, sewing last 1"/2.5cm at top of sleeve to armhole sts. Sew sleeve seams.

Sleeve edging

From RS, join C with a sl st in underarm seam. **Rnd 1** Ch 1, making sure that work lies flat, sc evenly around sleeve edge. Join rnd with a sl st in first st. **Rnd 2** Ch 1, sc in each st around. Join rnd with a sl st in first st. Fasten off.

SHORTS

LEFT LEG

With C, ch 52 (56, 62). **Row 1 (RS)** Hdc in 3rd ch from hook and in each ch across—50 (54, 60) sts. Ch 2, turn. Work in hdc and inc 1 st each side on next row, then every other row 2 (2, 3) times more, then

every row 5 (6, 6) times—66 (72, 80) sts.
Work even until piece measures 3 (3½,
4)"/7.5 (9, 10)cm from beg. Fasten off.
Turn work.

Crotch shaping

Next row Sk first 2 sts, join C with a hdc
in next st, work across to within last 2 sts.
Ch 2, turn—62 (68, 76) sts. Dec 1 st each
side every row 4 (5, 5) times—54 (58, 66)
sts. Work even until piece measures 11
(12, 12½)"/28 (30.5, 31.5)cm from beg.
Fasten off.

RIGHT LEG

Work as for left leg.

FINISHING

Sew front, back and leg seams. Measure
waist and add 1"/2.5cm. Cut elastic to
measurement. For casing for elastic, fold top
edge of shorts ¾"/2cm to WS and sew in
place leaving a 1"/2.5cm opening at center
back. Insert elastic through casing. Sew ends
of elastic tog. Sew opening closed.

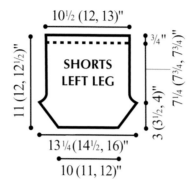

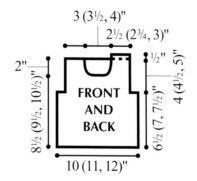

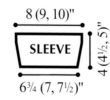

t a n k   g i r l

SIZES

Instructions are written for size 6 months. Changes for sizes 12 months and 18 months are in parentheses.

FINISHED MEASUREMENTS

Top
- Chest 20 (22, 24)"/51 (56, 61)cm
- Length 10 (11, 12)"/25.5 (28, 30.5)cm

Shorts
- Waist 21 (24, 26)"/53.5 (61, 66)cm
- Length 11 (12, 12½)"/28 (30.5, 31.5)cm

MATERIALS

Top
- 2 (3, 3) 1¾oz/50g balls (each approx 136yd/125m) of Patons Grace (cotton) in #60005 snow (A) **②**
- 1 ball each in #60134 royal (B) and #60705 cardinal (C)

Shorts
- 3 (3, 4) balls in #60705 cardinal (C)
- Size F/5 (3.75mm) crochet hook or size to obtain gauge
- Two ⅞"/22mm red star buttons
- ¾yd/.75m of ½"/13mm-wide elastic
- White sewing thread
- Sewing needle

GAUGE

20 sts and 17 rows to 4"/10cm over hdc using size F/5 (3.75mm) hook.
Take time to check gauge.

NOTE

See page 130 for working color changes for rows.

STRIPE PATTERN

Work 4 rows A in hdc and 2 rows B in sc. Rep these 6 rows for stripe pat.

TOP

BACK

With A, ch 52 (58, 62). **Row 1 (WS)** Hdc in 3rd ch from hook and in each ch across—50 (56, 60) sts. Ch 2, turn. **Rows 2-4** Hdc in each st across. Ch 2, turn. **Row 5** Rep row 2. Join B, ch 1, turn. **Rows 6 and 7** Sc in each st across. Ch 1, turn. When row 7 is completed, join A, ch 2, turn. Cont in stripe pat and work even until 4th B stripe has been completed. Cont with A and hdc until piece measures $6\frac{1}{2}$ (7, 8)"/16.5 (17.5, 20.5)cm from beg, end with a WS row. Fasten off. Turn work.

Armhole shaping

Next row Sk first 2 sts, join A with a hdc in next st, work across to within last 2 sts. Ch 2, turn—46 (52, 56) sts. Dec 1 st each side every row 3 (4, 4) times—40 (44, 48) sts. Work even until armhole measures $1\frac{1}{2}$ (2, $2\frac{1}{2}$)"/4 (5, 6.5)cm, end with a WS row.

Left neck shaping

Next row (RS) Work across first 17 (19, 21) sts, ch 2, turn. Dec 1 st from neck edge every row 5 (6, 7) times—12 (13, 14) sts. Work even until armhole measures 3$\frac{1}{2}$ (4, 4$\frac{1}{2}$)"/9 (10, 11.5)cm. Fasten off.

Right neck shaping

Next row (RS) Sk 6 center sts, join A with a hdc in next st, work to end. Cont to work as for left neck, reversing shaping.

FRONT

Work as for back.

FINISHING

Sew right shoulder seam.

Button band

From RS, join A with a sc in first st of left back shoulder, sc in next 11 (12, 13) sts. Ch 1, turn. Cont to work in sc for 2 more rows. Fasten off.

Buttonhole band

From RS, join A with a sc in first st of left front shoulder, sc in next 11 (12, 13) sts. Ch 1, turn. **Buttonhole row (WS)** Sc in first 1 (2, 2) sts, ch 2, sk next 2 sts, sc in next 5 (4, 5) sts, ch 2, sk next 2 sts, sc in last 1 (2, 2) sts. Ch 1, turn. **Next row** Sc across, working 2 sc in each ch-2 sp. Fasten off. Sew side seams.

Neck edging

From RS, join C with a sl st in side edge of left front buttonhole band. Making sure that work lies flat, sc evenly along entire neck edge. Ch 1, turn. **Next row** Sc in each st across. Fasten off.

Left armhole edging

From RS, join C with a sl st in side edge of left back button band. Making sure that work lies flat, sc evenly along entire armhole edge. Ch 1, turn. **Next row** Sc in each st across. Fasten off.

Right armhole edging

From RS, join C with a sl st in side seam. Making sure that work lies flat, sc evenly around armhole edge. Join rnd with a sl st in first st. Ch 1, turn. **Next rnd** Sc in each st around. Join rnd with a sl st in first st. Fasten off. Sew on buttons.

SHORTS

Left Leg

With C, ch 52 (56, 62). **Row 1 (RS)** Hdc in 3rd ch from hook and in each ch across—50 (54, 60) sts. Ch 2, turn. Work in hdc and inc 1 st each side on next row, then every other row 2 (2, 3) times more, then every row 5 (6, 6) times—66 (72, 80) sts. Work even until piece measures 3 (3½, 4)"/7.5 (9, 10)cm from beg. Fasten off. Turn work.

Crotch shaping

Next row Sk first 2 sts, join C with a hdc in next st, work across to within last 2 sts. Ch 2, turn—62 (68, 76) sts. Dec 1 st each side every row 4 (5, 5) times—54 (58, 66) sts. Work even until piece measures 11(12,12½)"/28 (30.5, 31.5)cm from beg. Fasten off.

RIGHT LEG

Work as for left leg.

FINISHING

Sew front, back and leg seams. Measure waist and add 1"/2.5cm. Cut elastic to measurement. For casing for elastic, fold top edge of shorts ¾"/2cm to WS and sew in place leaving a 1"/2.5cm opening at center back. Insert elastic through casing. Sew ends of elastic tog. Sew opening closed.

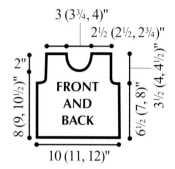

3 (3¾, 4)"
2½ (2½, 2¾)"
2"
8 (9, 10½)"
FRONT AND BACK
6½ (7, 8)"
3½ (4, 4½)"
10 (11, 12)"

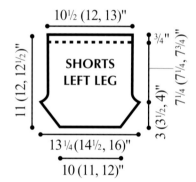

10½ (12, 13)"
¾"
11 (12, 12½)"
SHORTS LEFT LEG
3 (3½, 4)"
7¼ (7¼, 7¾)"
13¼ (14½, 16)"
10 (11, 12)"

SIZE

Instructions are written for size 6 months.

FINISHED MEASUREMENTS

- Chest (closed) 20"/51cm
- Length 9¹/₂"/24cm
- Upper arm 6"/15cm

MATERIALS

- 2 1³/₄oz/50g balls (each approx 151yd/138m) of Rowan Yarns Kid Classic (lambswool/mohair/nylon) in #819 pinched (MC) (4)
- 1 ball in #833 cherish (CC)
- Size H/8 (5mm) crochet hook or size to obtain gauge
- Yarn needle

GAUGE

12 sts and 14 rows to 4"/10cm over pat st using size H/8 (5mm) hook.
Take time to check gauge.

NOTE

Sweater is made in one piece.

PATTERN STITCH

Row 1 *Sc in next dc, dc in next sc; rep from * to end. Ch 1, turn.
Rep row 1 for pat st.

BODY

Back

Beg at back bottom edge, with MC, ch 31.
Foundation row (RS) Sc in 2nd ch from hook, dc in next ch, *sc in next ch, dc in next ch; rep from * to end—30 sts. Ch 1, turn. Cont in pat st and work even until piece measures 6¹/₂"/16.5cm from beg, end with a WS row. Fasten off. Turn work.

Sleeves

Next row (RS) With MC, ch 18, cont in pat st across 30 back sts. Ch 19, turn. **Next row** Sc in 2nd ch from hook, dc in next st, [sc in next ch, dc in next ch] 8 times, cont in pat st across 30 back sts, [sc in next ch, dc in next ch] 9 times—66 sts. Ch 1, turn. Work even until sleeve measures 3"/7.5cm from beg, end with a WS row.

Right neck shaping

Next row (RS) Work across first 30 sts. Ch 1, turn. **Note:** In order to maintain pat st when shaping, work as foll: when the last st worked is a sc, the first st on the next row will be a dc, so you must ch 3 (instead of ch 1) before turning. Dec 1 st at beg of next row, then at same edge every row once more—28 sts. Work even for 2 rows. Inc 1 st at neck edge on next row, then every row 4 times more—33 sts. Work even until sleeve measures 6"/15cm, end with a RS row.

Right front

Next row (WS) Work across first 15 sts; leave rem 18 sts unworked for end of sleeve. Ch 3, turn. Cont in pat st for 6¹/₂"/16.5cm. Fasten off.

Left neck shaping

Next row (RS) Sk 6 center sts, join MC with a sc in next st, work to end. Ch 1, turn—30 sts. Cont to work as for right front, reversing shaping.

FINISHING

Sew side and sleeve seams

Embroidery

Use a single strand of CC in yarn needle. On RS, embroider a row of blanket stitches around fronts, neck and bottom edges. For sleeves, embroider blanket stitches on WS. Fold back cuffs; as shown.

Ties

(make 2)

With MC, make a ch that measures 10"/25.5cm-long. **Row 1** Sl st in 2nd ch from hook and in each ch across. Fasten off leaving a long tail for sewing. Sew ties at beg of neck shaping.

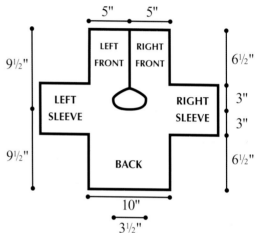

Instructions are written for size 6 months. Changes for sizes 12 months and 18 months are in parentheses.

FINISHED MEASUREMENTS

- Chest (buttoned) 22 (24, 26)"/56 (61, 66)cm
- Length 11 (12, 13)"/28 (30.5, 33)cm
- Upper arm 9 (10, 11)"/23 (25.5, 28)cm

MATERIALS

- *4 (5, 5) 1³/₄oz/50g balls (each approx 136yd/125m) of Debbie Bliss KFI Cashmerino Baby (wool/microfiber) in #608 lavender* 🧶 **3**
- *Size G/6 (4mm) crochet hook or size to obtain gauge*
- *Five ¹/₂"/13mm buttons*
- *2yd/2m of ³/₄"/19mm-wide ecru cotton lace*
- *Ecru sewing thread*
- *Sewing needle*

GAUGE

16 sts and 12 rows to 4"/10cm over hdc using size G/6 (4mm) hook.
Take time to check gauge.

BACK

Ch 46 (50, 54). **Row 1 (WS)** Hdc in 3rd ch from hook and in each ch across—44 (48, 52) sts. Ch 2, turn. **Row 2** Hdc in each st across. Ch 2, turn. Rep row 2 for pat st and work even until piece measures 6¹/₂ (7, 7¹/₂)"/16.5 (17.5, 19)cm from beg, end with a WS row. Fasten off. Turn work.

Armhole shaping

Next row (RS) Sk first 4 sts, join yarn with a hdc in next st, work across to within last 4 sts. Ch 2, turn—36 (40, 44) sts. Work even until armhole measures 4¹/₂ (5, 5¹/₂)"/11.5 (12.5, 14)cm. Fasten off.

LEFT FRONT

Ch 22 (24, 26). **Row 1 (WS)** Hdc in 3rd ch from hook and in each ch across—20 (22, 24) sts. Ch 2, turn. Work even in hdc until piece measures 6$\frac{1}{2}$ (7, 7$\frac{1}{2}$)"/16.5 (17.5, 19)cm from beg, end with a WS row. Fasten off. Turn work.

Armhole shaping

Next row (RS) Sk first 4 sts, join yarn with a hdc in next st, work to end. Ch 2, turn—16 (18, 20) sts. Work even until armhole measures 2$\frac{1}{2}$ (3, 3)"/6.5 (7.5, 7.5)cm, end with a WS row.

Neck shaping

Next row (RS) Work across first 13 (15, 17) sts. Ch 2, turn. Dec 1 st at neck edge on next row, then every other row twice more—10 (12, 14) sts. Work even until same length as back. Fasten off.

RIGHT FRONT

Work as for left front reversing shaping.

SLEEVES

Ch 26 (30, 32). **Row 1 (WS)** Hdc in 3rd ch from hook and in each ch across—24 (28, 30) sts. Ch 2, turn. Work in hdc and inc 1 st each side on next row, then every 4th row 5 (5, 6) times more—36 (40, 44) sts. Work even until piece measures 8 (9, 10)"/20.5 (23, 25.5)cm from beg. Fasten off.

FINISHING

Sew shoulder seams.

Neck edging

From RS, join yarn with a sc in first st of right neck shaping. **Row 1** Making sure that work lies flat, sc evenly along entire neck edge. Ch 1, turn. **Rows 2 and 3** Sc in each st across, dec 1 st at each shoulder seam. Ch 1, turn. After row 3 is completed, fasten off.

Button band

From RS, join yarn with a sc in side edge of left neck edging. **Row 1** Making sure that work lies flat, sc evenly along entire front edge. Ch 1, turn. **Rows 2-4** Sc in each st across. Ch 1, turn. After row 4 is completed, fasten off. Place markers on band for 5 buttons, with the first ½"/1.5cm from neck edge, the last ½"/1.5cm from bottom edge and the rest spaced evenly between.

Buttonhole band

From RS, join yarn with a sc in side edge of right front. **Row 1** Making sure that work lies flat, sc evenly along entire front edge. Ch 1, turn. **Row 2** Sc in each st across. Ch 1, turn. **Row 3 (buttonhole row)** *Sc in each st to marker, ch 2, sk next 2 sts; rep from * to end. Ch 1, turn.

Row 4 Sc across, working 2 sc in each ch-2 sp. Fasten off. Set in sleeves, sewing last 1"/2.5cm at top of sleeve to armhole sts. Sew side and sleeve seams. Sew on buttons.

Lace trim

Refer to photo. For first row of lace on left front, measure from 1/4"/.6cm above top edge of 3rd button to 1"/2.5cm from beg of armhole. Cut lace 1"/2.5cm longer than measurement. Turn side edges under 1/2"/1.3cm to wrong side and press. Sew on lace. Rep on right front. For 3rd row of lace, measure from bottom edge of 5th button to top shoulder/sleeve seam. Cut and sew on lace, then rep on right front. On each front, center 2nd row of lace between first and 3rd rows, then use same spacing to sew on 4th row of lace.

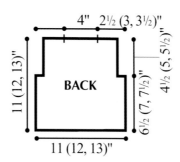

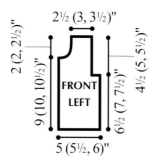

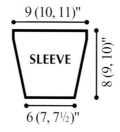

SIZES

Instructions are written for size 6 months. Changes for sizes 12 months and 18 months are in parentheses.

FINISHED MEASUREMENTS

• Waist 20 (22, 24)"/51 (56, 61)cm
• Hem 28 (30, 34)"/71 (76, 86.5)cm

MATERIALS

• 2 6oz/170g skeins (each approx 290yd/265m) of TLC Coats & Clark Amore (acrylic/nylon) in #3710 rose ⑤
• Size H/8 (5mm) crochet hook or size to obtain gauge
• ¾yd/.75m of ½"/13mm-wide elastic
• White sewing thread
• Sewing needle
• Two safety pins
• Iron-on flower applique

GAUGE

14 sts and 16 rows to 4"/10cm over sc using size H/8 (5mm) hook.
Take time to check gauge.

BIB

Ch 15 (17, 19). **Row 1** Sc in 2nd ch from hook and in each ch across—14 (16, 18) sts. Ch 1, turn. **Row 2** Sc in each st across. Ch 1, turn. Rep row 2 for pat st and work even until piece measures 4 (4½, 5)"/10 (11.5, 12.5)cm from beg. Fasten off.

SKIRT

Beg at waist, ch 71 (79, 85). **Row 1** Sc in 2nd ch from hook and in each ch across—70 (78, 84) sts. Ch 1, turn. Work even in sc until piece measures 2"/5cm from beg. **Next row** Inc 28 (28, 36) sts evenly spaced across—98 (106, 120) sts. Work even until piece measures 10 (11, 12)"/25.5 (28, 30.5)cm from beg. Fasten off.

STRAPS

(make 2)
Ch 5. **Row 1** Sc in 2nd ch from hook and in each ch across—4 sts. Ch 1, turn. Work even in sc until piece measures 14"/35.5cm from beg. Cut yarn, but do not fasten off. Fasten safety pin in lp to prevent work from unraveling.

FINISHING

Sew back seam of skirt. Measure waist and add 1"/2.5cm. Cut elastic to measurement. For casing for elastic, fold top edge of skirt 1"/2.5cm to WS and sew in place leaving a 1"/2.5cm opening at center back. Insert elastic through casing. Sew ends of elastic tog. Sew opening closed. Sew bib to center front of skirt waist. Sew bottom edge of straps to top edge of bib. Try dress on baby, then adjust length of straps so straps meet top edge of waist; fasten off each strap. Sew straps to back waist edge. Adhere appliqué to bib following package directions.

20 (22, 24)"

1"
1"

10 (11, 12)"

SKIRT

8 (9, 10)"

28 (30, 34)"

BIB

4 (4½, 5)"

4 (4½, 5)"

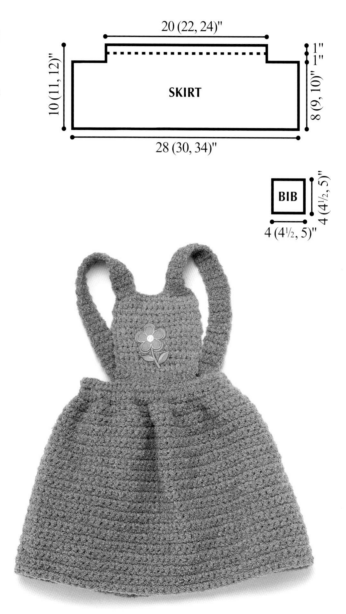

CARDIGAN

SIZES

Instructions are written for size 6 months. Changes for sizes 12 months and 18 months are in parentheses.

FINISHED MEASUREMENTS

- Chest (buttoned) 22 (24, 26)"/56 (61, 66)cm
- Length 11 (12, 13)"/28 (30.5, 33)cm
- Upper arm 9 (10, 11)"/23 (25.5, 28)cm

MATERIALS

- *3 (4, 5) 1³/₄oz/50g balls (each approx 136yd/125m) of Patons Grace (cotton) in #60005 snow* (3)
- *Size G/6 (4mm) crochet hook or size to obtain gauge*
- *Five ⁵/₈"/16mm cover-your-own button blanks*
- *¹/₄yd/.25m of blue gingham fabric*
- *One skein of six-strand embroidery floss in medium blue*
- *Embroidery needle*
- *Sewing needle*
- *White sewing thread*
- *Straight pins*

GAUGE

18 sts and 16 rows to 4"/10cm over hdc using size G/6 (4mm) hook.
Take time to check gauge.

BACK

Ch 52 (56, 60). **Row 1 (RS)** Hdc in 3rd ch from hook and in each ch across—50 (54, 58) sts. Ch 2, turn. **Row 2** Hdc in each st across. Ch 2, turn. Rep row 2 for pat st and work even until piece measures 11 (12, 13)"/28 (30.5, 33)cm from beg. Fasten off.

LEFT FRONT

Ch 24 (26, 29). **Row 1 (RS)** Hdc in 3rd ch from hook and in each ch across—22 (24, 27) sts. Ch 2, turn. Work even in hdc until piece measures 8¹/₂ (9, 10)"/21.5 (23, 25.5)cm from beg, end with a WS row.
Neck shaping
Next row (RS) Work across to within last 3 (3, 4) sts. Ch 1, turn—19 (21, 23) sts. Dec 1 st at neck edge on next row, then every row 3 times more—15 (17, 19) sts. Work even until same length as back. Fasten off.

RIGHT FRONT

Work as for left front reversing neck shaping.

SLEEVES

Ch 29 (31, 33). **Row 1 (RS)** Sc in 2nd ch from hook and in each ch across—28 (30, 32) sts. Ch 2, turn. Work in hdc and inc 1 st each side on next row, then every 3rd row 6 (7, 8) times more—42 (46, 50) sts. Work even until piece measures 7 (8, 9)"/17.5 (20.5, 23)cm from beg. Fasten off.

FINISHING

Sew shoulder seams.

Neck edging

From RS, join yarn with a sc in first st of right neck shaping. **Row 1** Making sure that work lies flat, sc evenly along entire neck edge. Ch 1, turn. **Row 2** Sc in each st across, dec 1 st at each shoulder seam. Fasten off.

Button band

From RS, join yarn with a sc in side edge of left neck edging. **Row 1** Making sure that work lies flat, sc evenly along entire front edge. Ch 1, turn. **Rows 2 and 3** Sc in each st across. Ch 1, turn. After row 3 is completed, fasten off. Place markers on band for 5 buttons, with the first 1/2"/1.5cm from neck edge, the last 1/2"/1.5cm from bottom edge and the rest spaced evenly between.

Buttonhole band

From RS, join yarn with a sc in side edge of right front. **Row 1** Making sure that work lies flat, sc evenly along entire front edge. Ch 1, turn. **Row 2 (buttonhole row)** *Sc in each st to marker, ch 2, sk next 2 sts; rep from * to end. Ch 1, turn. **Row 3** Sc across, working 2 sc in each ch-2 sp. Fasten off. Place markers 4$\frac{1}{2}$ (5, 5$\frac{1}{2}$)"/11.5 (12.5, 14)cm down from shoulder seams on front and back. Sew sleeves to armholes between markers. Sew side and sleeve seams. Cover buttons with fabric following package directions. Sew on buttons.

Bow

Cut eight 4" x 8"/10cm x 20.5cm pieces of fabric. Place two pairs of fabric pieces tog, RS facing. Using a $\frac{1}{2}$"/1.5cm seam allowance throughout, sew across one short edge and both long edges. Clip corners, turn RS out and press. For right bow loop, trim unsewn short edge so loop now measures 4"/10cm-long. Turn short edge $\frac{1}{2}$"/1.5cm to inside and press. At this same edge, make an inverted pleat, then tack in place to secure. Pin bow loop to right front so pleated edge butts first row of buttonhole band and top edge butts first row of neck edging. For left bow loop, work same as for right.

For streamers, place two pairs of fabric pieces tog, RS facing. Sew across each long edge and sew one short edge into a 2"/5cm-deep "V" for points. Trim away excess fabric at "V" to within $\frac{1}{4}$"/6mm of stitching. Clip corners and "V". Turn RS out and press. For right streamer, trim unsewn short edge so streamer now measures 6"/15cm-long. At this same edge, make an inverted pleat, then tack in place to secure. Pin streamer to right front, tucking pleated edge $\frac{1}{2}$"/1.5cm under right bow loop; as shown. For left streamer, work as for right, but trim length so streamer now measures 5"/12.5cm-long. Pin streamer to left front, tucking pleated edge $^1/_2$"/1.5cm under left bow loop; as shown. Using all six strands of floss in embroidery needle and working in blanket stitch, sew streamers in place first, then sew loops.

For bow knot, cut a 2"/5cm square of fabric. Along opposite edges, fold $^1/_2$"/1.5cm to WS and press. Fold one raw edge $^3/_4$"/2cm to WS, then fold opposite raw edge $^1/_2$"/1.5cm to WS; tack in place to secure. Butt knot against pleated edge of left bow loop as shown, then sew in place using thread.

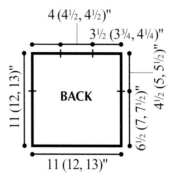

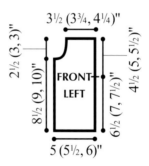

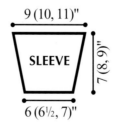

DRESS

SIZES

Instructions are written for size 6 months. Changes for sizes 12 months and 18 months are in parentheses.

FINISHED MEASUREMENTS

- Chest 18 (20, 22)"/45.5 (51, 56)cm
- Length 14 (16, 19)"/35.5 (40.5, 48)cm

MATERIALS

- *3 (4, 5) 1³/₄oz/50g balls (each approx 136yd/125m) of Patons Grace (cotton) in #60130 sky* (**3**)
- *Size F/5 (3.75mm) crochet hook or size to obtain gauge*
- *1¹/₄yd/1.25m of ³/₈"/10mm-wide blue gingham ribbon*

GAUGE

20 sts and 20 rows to 4"/10cm over pat st using size F/5 (3.75mm) hook.
Take time to check gauge.

NOTES

1) Back and front bodices are made separately, then sewn tog.
2) Skirt is made in one piece from bodice to hem.

PATTERN STITCH

Row 1 *Sc in front lp of next st, sc in back lp of next st; rep from * to end. Ch 1, turn. Rep row 1 for pat st.

BACK BODICE

Ch 47 (51, 57). **Foundation row** Sc in 2nd ch from hook and in each ch across—46 (50, 56) sts. Ch 1, turn. Cont in pat st and work even until piece measures 2 (2¹/₂, 3)"/5 (6.5, 7.5)cm from beg. Fasten off. Turn work.

Armhole shaping

Next row Sk first 3 (3, 4) sts, join yarn with a sc in next st, work in pat st as established to within last 3 (3, 4) sts. Ch 1, turn—40 (44, 48) sts. Dec 1 st each side on next row, then every row 1 (1, 2) times more—36 (40, 42) sts. Work even until armhole measures 1 (1¹/₂, 2)"/2.5 (4, 5)cm.

Left neck shaping

Next row Work across first 14 (16, 17) sts, ch 1, turn. Dec 1 st at beg of next row, then at same edge every row 3 (4, 2) times more, every other row 0 (0, 2) times—10 (11, 12) sts. Work even until armhole measures 3 (3¹/₂, 4)"/7.5 (9, 10)cm. Fasten off.

Right neck shaping

Next row (RS) Sk 8 center sts, join yarn with a sc in next st, work to end. Cont to work as for left neck, reversing shaping.

FRONT BODICE

Work as for back bodice. Sew shoulder and side seams.

SKIRT

From RS, join yarn with a sl st in right side seam. **Rnd 1** Ch 1, working through bottom lps of foundation row, work 2 sc in each st around—92 (100, 112) sts. Join rnd with a sl st in first st. **Rnd 2** Ch 1, *work 2 sc in next st, sc in next st; rep from * around—138 (150, 168) sts. Join rnd with a sl st in first st. **Rnd 3** Ch 2, hdc in each st around. Join rnd with a sl st in first st. Rep rnd 3 for pat st and work even until skirt measures 9 (10, 12)"/23 (25.5, 30.5)cm from beg. Fasten off.

FINISHING

Neck edging

From RS, join yarn with a sc in center back neck edge. **Rnd 1** Ch 1, making sure that work lies flat, sc evenly around neck edge. Join rnd with a sl st in first sc. Fasten off.

Armhole edging

From RS, join yarn with a sc in underarm seam. **Rnd 1** Ch 1, making sure that work lies flat, sc evenly around armhole edge. Join rnd with a sl st in first sc. Fasten off. Weave ribbon through rnd 3 of skirt, beg and ending at center front. Tie ribbon in a bow and trim ends at an angle.

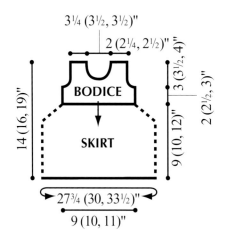

SIZES

Instructions are written for size 6-12 months. Changes for size 12-18 months are in parentheses.

MATERIALS

• *1³⁄₄oz/50g balls of sportweight yarn in wool or wool blend* (3)

Dinosaurs

• *1 ball in bright green (MC)*

Bears

• *1 ball in medium brown (MC) and 5yd/5m each in off white (A) and black (B)*

Bunnies

• *1 ball in pink (MC) and 5yd/5m in white (CC)*

Ducks

• *1 ball in yellow (MC), 5yd/5m in orange (A) and 1yd/1m in black (B)*

• *For size 6-12 months, size F/5 (3.75mm) crochet hook or size to obtain gauge*

• *For size 12-18 months, size G/6 (4mm) crochet hook or size to obtain gauge*

• *One small safety pin*

• *Yarn needle*

• *Four 8mm sew-on wiggle eyes for each pair of booties*

GAUGES

• 16 sts and 19 rows to 4"/10cm over sc using size F/5 (3.75mm) hook.
• 14 sts and 17 rows to 4"/10cm over sc using size G/6 (4mm) hook.
Take time to check gauges.

BASIC BOOTIE

Beg at center bottom of sole, with size F/3.75mm (G/4mm) hook and MC, ch 14.

Rnd 1 Sc in 2nd ch from hook, sc in next 9 ch, hdc in next ch, work 2 hdc in next ch, 3 hdc in last ch. Turn to bottom lps of beg ch. Work 2 hdc in each of first 2 lps, hdc in next lp, sc in next 9 lps, work 2 sc in last lp—32 sts. Mark last st made with the safety pin. You will be working in a spiral (to rnd 12) marking the last st made with the safety pin to indicate end of rnd.

Rnd 2 Work 2 sc in next st, sc in next 12 sts, [work 2 sc in next st, sc in next st] 3 times, sc in next 11 sts, 2 sc in next st, sc in next st—37 sts.

Rnd 3 Work 2 sc in next st, sc in next 13 sts, [work 2 sc in next st, sc in next st] twice, [sc in next st, 2 sc in next st] twice, sc in next 13 sts, work 2 sc in next st, sc in next st—43 sts.

Rnd 4 Working in back lps only, sc in each st around.

Rnd 5 Sc in each st around.

Rnd 6 Sc in next 16 sts, [dec 1 st over next 2 sts, sc in next st] 4 times, sc in next 15 sts—39 sts.

Rnd 7 Sc in next 15 sts, [dec 1 st over next 2 sts] 5 times, sc in next 14 sts—34 sts.

Rnd 8 Sc in next 14 sts, hdc in next 2 sts, working in hdc, dec 1 st over next 2 sts, hdc in next 2 sts, sc in next 14 sts—33 sts.

Rnd 9 Sc in next 14 sts, hdc in next 2 sts, working in hdc, dec 1 st over next 2 sts, hdc in next 2 sts, sc in next 14 sts—32 sts.

Rnd 10 Sc in next 14 sts, [working in hdc, dec 1 st over next 2 sts] twice, sc in next 14 sts—30 sts.

Rnd 11 Sc in next 11 sts, [working in sc, dec 1 st over next 2 sts] 3 times, sc next 11 sts—27 sts. Drop safety pin. Join rnd with a sl st in next st. Ch 2, turn.

Rnds 12, 13, 14 and 15 Hdc in each st around. Join rnd with a sl st in first st. Ch 2, turn. After rnd 15 is completed, do not ch, fasten off.

DINOSAURS

Using MC, make 2 basic booties.

Scales

(make 4)

With MC, ch 10. **Row 1** Sc in 2nd ch from hook, [work (hdc, 2 dc, hdc) in next ch, sk next ch, sc in next ch] once more, end work (hdc, 2 dc, hdc) in next ch, sl st in last ch. Fasten off leaving a long tail for sewing.

FINISHING

Sew a scale to front and back of each bootie; as shown. Sew on eyes.

BEARS

Using MC, make 2 basic booties.

Ears

(make 4)

With A, ch 4. Join ch with a sl st forming a ring. **Row 1** Work 6 sc over ring. Change to MC, ch 3, turn. **Row 2** Dc in first 2 sts, work 2 dc in each of next 2 sts, dc in last 2 sts. Fasten off leaving a long tail for sewing.

FINISHING

Sew on ears and eyes.

Embroidery

Use a single strand of B in yarn needle. Embroider nose in satin stitch, lip in straight stitch and mouth in stem stitch; as shown.

BUNNIES

Using MC, make 2 basic booties.

Ears

(make 4)

With CC, ch 10. **Row 1** Sc in 2nd ch from hook and in next 7 ch, work 5 sc in last ch. Turn to bottom lps of beg ch. Sk first lp, sc in each of 8 lps. Join MC, ch 2, turn. **Row 2** Hdc in first 10 sts, work 3 hdc in next st, hdc in last 10 sts. Fasten off leaving a long tail for sewing.

FINISHING

Sew on ears and eyes.

Embroidery

Use a single strand of CC in yarn needle. Embroider nose in satin stitch; as shown.

Tails

Using MC, make two 2"/5cm in diameter pompoms (see pompom instructions). Sew a pompom to back of each bootie, as shown.

DUCKS

Using MC, make 2 basic booties.

Bills

(make 2)

With A, ch 7. **Row 1 (WS)** Sc in 2nd ch from hook and in each ch across—6 sts. Ch 1, turn. **Row 2** Working in sc, dec 1 st over first 2 sts, sc in next 2 sts, dec 1 st over last 2 sts—4 sts. Ch 1, turn. **Row 3** Working in sc, [dec 1 st over next 2 sts] twice—2 sts. Fasten off. **Edging** From RS, join A with a sc in side edge of row 1. Making sure that work lies flat, sc evenly around edge to row 1 on opposite side. Fasten off leaving a long tail for sewing.

FINISHING

Sew on eyes.

Embroidery

Use a single strand of B in yarn needle. Embroider nostrils in straight stitch as shown. Sew on bills; as shown.

THE SLIP KNOT

1 Begin to crochet by making a slip knot. Make a loop several inches [or centimeters] from the end of the yarn. Insert the hook through the loop and catch the tail with the end.

2 Pull the yarn through the loop on the hook.

CROCHET HOOKS

US	METRIC
14 steel	.60mm
12 steel	.75mm
10 steel	1.00mm
6 steel	1.50mm
5 steel	1.75mm
B/1	2.25mm
C/2	2.75mm
D/3	3.25mm
E/4	3.50mm
F/5	3.75mm
G/6	4.00mm
H/8	5.00mm
I/9	5.50mm
J/10	6.00mm
K/10.5	6.50mm
L/11	8.00mm

YARN SELECTION

For an exact reproduction of the projects photographed, use the yarn listed in the "Materials" section of the pattern. We've chosen yarns that are readily available in the U.S. and Canada at the time of printing. The Resources list on page 144 provides addresses of yarn distributors. Contact them for the name of a retailer in your area.

YARN SUBSTITUTION

You may wish to substitute yarns. Perhaps you view small-scale projects as a chance to incorporate leftovers from your yarn stash, or the yarn specified may not be available in your area. You'll need to crochet to the given gauge to obtain the crocheted measurements with a substitute yarn (see "Gauge" on this page). Be sure to consider how the fiber content of the substitute yarn will affect the comfort and the ease of care of your projects.

To facilitate yarn substitution, yarns are graded by the standard stitch gauge obtained in single crochet. You'll find a grading number in the "Materials" section of the pattern, immediately following the fiber type of the yarn. Look for a substitute yarn that falls into the same category. The suggested hook size and gauge on the yarn label should be comparable to that on the "Standard Yarn Weight System" chart (see page 131).

After you've successfully gauge-swatched a substitute yarn, you'll need to figure out how much of the substitute yarn the project requires. First, find the total length of the original yarn in the pattern (multiply number of balls by yards/meters per ball). Divide this figure by the new yards/meters per ball (listed on the yarn label). Round up to the next whole number. The answer is the number of balls required.

GAUGE

It is always important to crochet a gauge swatch, and it is even more so with garments to ensure proper fit.

Patterns usually state gauge over a 4"/10cm span, however it's beneficial to make a larger test swatch. This gives a more precise stitch gauge, a better idea of the appearance and drape of the crocheted fabric, and gives you a chance to familiarize yourself with the stitch pattern.

The type of hook used—wood, plastic or metal—will influence gauge, so crochet your swatch with the hook you plan to use for the project. Try different hook sizes until your sample measures the required number of stitches and rows. To get fewer stitches to the inch/cm, use a larger hook; to get more stitches to the inch/cm, use a smaller hook.

It's a good idea to keep your gauge swatch in order to test blocking and cleaning methods.

FOLLOWING CHARTS

Charts are a convenient way to follow colorwork patterns at a glance. When crocheting back and forth in rows, read charts from right to left on right side (RS) rows and from left to right on wrong side (WS) rows, repeating any stitch and row repeats as directed in the pattern. Posting a self-adhesive note under your working row is an easy way to keep track of your place.

COLORWORK CROCHETING

Two main types of colorwork are explored in this book: stripes and stranding.

Stripes

When working in single crochet, change color by drawing the new color through 2 loops on hook to complete the last single crochet, then working the next stitch with the new color, or, if at the end of the row, chain and turn.

For half double crochet, draw new color through 3 loops on hook to complete last half double crochet, work the next stitch with the new color, or, if at the end of the row, chain and turn.

When working in double crochet, draw new color through last 2 loops on hook to complete last double crochet, work the next stitch with the new color, or, if at the end of the row, chain and turn.

To prevent lumpy seams, do not make knots when changing colors. Instead, leave a long tail of yarn, then weave in tails after piece is completed and before sewing blocks together.

Stranding

When changing colors at the beginning of rows or rounds, carry yarn along for a few rows only, or cut yarn and rejoin when needed. It is important to keep the floats small and neat so they don't catch on small fingers when the garment is pulled on.

When changing colors, pick up new color from under dropped color to prevent holes.

BLOCKING

Blocking is a crucial finishing step in the crocheting process. It is the best way to shape pattern pieces and smooth crocheted edges in preparation for sewing together. Most designs retain their shape if the blocking stages in the instructions are followed carefully. Choose a blocking method according to the instructions on the yarn care label, and when in doubt, test-block your gauge swatch.

Wet Block Method

Using rust-proof pins, pin pieces to measurements on a flat surface and lightly dampen using a spray bottle. Allow to dry before removing pins.

CHAIN

1 Pass yarn over the hook and catch it with the hook.

2 Draw yarn through the loop on the hook.

3 Repeat steps 1 and 2 to make a chain.

STRAIGHT STITCH

BLANKET STITCH

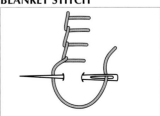

STANDARD YARN WEIGHT SYSTEM						
Categories of yarn, gauge ranges and recommended needle and hook sizes						
Yarn Weight Symbol & Category Names	**1** **Super Fine**	**2** **Fine**	**3** **Light**	**4** **Medium**	**5** **Bulky**	**6** **Super Bulky**
Type of Yarns in Category	Sock, Fingering, Baby	Sport, Baby	DK, Light Worsted	Worsted, Afghan, Aran	Chunky, Craft, Rug	Super Bulky, Roving
Knit Gauge Range* in Stockinette Stitch to 4 inches	27–32 sts	23–26 sts	21–24 sts	16–20 sts	12–15 sts	6–11 sts
Recommended Needle in Metric Size Range	2.25–3.25 mm	3.25–3.75 mm	3.75–4.5 mm	4.5–5.5 mm	5.5–8 mm	9–15 mm and larger
Recommended Needle U.S. size range	1 to 3	3 to 5	5 to 7	7 to 9	9 to 11	11 to 19 and larger
Crochet Gauge* Ranges in Single Crochet to 4 inch	21–32 sts	16–20 sts	12–17 sts	11–14 sts	8–11 sts	5–9 sts
Recommended Hook in Metric Size Range	2.25–3.5 mm	3.5–4.5 mm	4.5–5.5 mm	5.5–6.5 mm	6.5–9 mm	9–12 mm and larger
Recommended Hook U.S. Size Range	B-1 to E-4	E-4 to 7	7 to I-9	I-9 to K-10½	K-10½ to M-13	M-13 to P-16 and larger

* GUIDELINES ONLY: The above reflect the most commonly used gauges and needle or hook sizes for specific yarn categories.

SINGLE CROCHET

1 Insert hook through top two loops of a stitch. Pass yarn over hook and draw up a loop—two loops on hook.

2 Pass yarn over hook and draw through both loops on hook.

3 Continue in the same way, inserting hook into each stitch.

RUNNING STITCH

Steam Block Method

With wrong sides facing, pin pieces. Steam lightly, holding the iron 2"/5cm above the piece. Do not press or it will flatten stitches.

CARE

Refer to the yarn label for the recommended cleaning method. Many of the projects in the book can be either washed by hand, or in the machine on a gentle or wool cycle, using lukewarm water with a mild detergent. Do not agitate or soak for more than 10 minutes. Rinse gently with tepid water, then fold in a towel and gently press the water out. Lay flat to dry, away from excess heat and light. Check the yarn label for any specific care instructions such as dry cleaning or tumble drying.

FRINGE

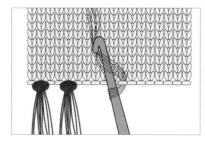

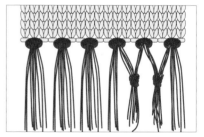

Simple fringe: Cut yarn twice desired length plus extra for knotting. On wrong side, insert hook from front to back through piece and over folded yarn. Pull yarn through. Draw ends through and tighten. Trim yarn.

Knotted fringe: After working a simple fringe (it should be longer to allow for extra knotting), take one half of the strands from each fringe and knot them with half the strands from the neighboring fringe.

MAKING POMPOMS

POMPOM TEMPLATE

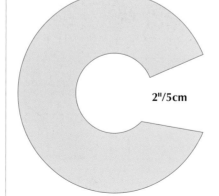

2"/5cm

1 Following the template, cut two circular pieces of cardboard.

2 Place tie strand between the circles. Wrap yarn around circles. Cut between circles

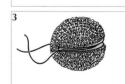

3 Knot tie strand tightly. Remove cardboard.

4 Place pompom between 2 smaller cardboard circles held together with a long needle and trim edges.

Note: For the safety and protection of your child, it is important to secure all pompoms and bobbles to the baby garment design. We recommend firmly tugging each pompom and bobble after each one is sewn on to ensure that they're secure.

CROCHETING GLOSSARY

decrease 1 dc [Yo. Insert hook into next st and draw up a lp. Yo and draw through 2 lps] twice, yo and draw through all 3 lps on hook.

decrease 1 hdc [Yo, insert hook into next st and draw up a lp] twice, yo and draw through all 5 lps on hook.

decrease 1 sc [Insert hook into next st and draw up a lp] twice, yo and draw through all 3 lps on hook.

increase 1 stitch Work 2 sts in 1 st.

join yarn with a dc Make a slip knot, then yo. Insert hook into st. Yo and draw up a lp. [Yo and draw through 2 lps on hook] twice.

join yarn with a hdc Make a slip knot, then yo. Insert hook into st. Yo and draw up a lp. Yo and draw through 3 lps on hook.

join yarn with a sc Make a slip knot. Insert hook into st. Yo and draw up a lp. Yo and draw through 2 lps on hook.

join yarn with a sl st Make a slip knot. Insert hook into st. Yo and draw up a lp and draw through lp on hook.

CROCHET ABBREVIATIONS

approx approximately
beg begin(ning)
CC contrasting color
ch chain(s)
cont continu(e)(ing)
dc double crochet (UK: tr treble)
dec decrease(ing) (see glossary)
g gram(s)
hdc half double crochet (UK: htr half treble)
inc increas(e)(ing) (see glossary)

lp(s) loop(s)
m meter(s)
mm millimeter(s)
MC main color
oz ounce(s)
pat(s) pattern(s)
rem remain(s)(ing)
rep repeat
rnd(s) round(s)
RS right side(s)
sc single crochet (UK: dc double crochet)
sk skip
sl slip
sl st slip st (UK: sc single crochet)
st(s) stitch(es)

tog together
tr treble crochet (UK: dtr double treble)
WS wrong side(s)
yd yard(s)
yo yarn over
* = repeat directions following * as many times as indicated.
[ ] = repeat directions inside brackets as many times as indicated.
( ) = work directions contained inside parentheses in st indicated.

HALF-DOUBLE CROCHET

1 Pass yarn over hook. Insert hook through the top two loops of a stitch.

2 Pass yarn over hook and draw up a loop—three loops on hook. Pass yarn over hook.

3 Draw through all three loops on hook.

STEM STITCH

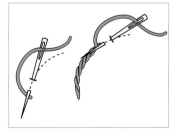

SATIN STITCH

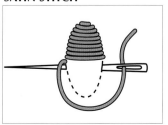

DOUBLE CROCHET

1 Pass yarn over hook. Insert hook through the top two loops of a stitch.

2 Pass yarn over hook and draw up a loop—three loops on hook.

3 Pass yarn over hook and draw it through the first two loops on the hook, pass yarn over hook and draw through the remaining two loops. Continue in the same way, inserting hook into each stitch.

There are many people who help make a book happen. First, I'd like to thank my top-notch crocheter and project manager supreme, Joyce Nordstrom. She worked long hours on tight deadlines and always came through when I needed her. Joyce, you are my savior.

Thank you to Judy Timmer and Jane Lind for their expert crocheting and dedication to helping me complete my projects.

a c k n o w l e d g m e n t s

Behind every designer is a supportive team. I want to thank my mom Jean and my sister Rajeana for understanding that I really was too busy to come out and play; my daughter Heather and my son Jonathan for giving me hugs and kisses when I needed them most; and my husband Tom Noggle for respecting my space and knowing when to make me laugh. And last but not least, my grandson Johnny for always smiling when he sees me.

Finally, I want to thank everyone at Sixth&Spring Books for making this possible: Michelle Lo, for prodding just when she needed to and never pushing too hard—without her, I would still be spinning around in my chair trying to get organized; Chi Ling Moy for the beautiful book design, art direction and ability to hide any flaws; Pat Harste for working her magic on my patterns (she really is the best); and of course, Dan Howell, Mary Helt, Carla Scott and Stefanie Carrea for all their hard work. Lastly, thank you to Trisha Malcolm, who always believed in me—I consider her a true friend.

r e s o u r c e s

Berroco, Inc.
14 Elmdale Road
PO Box 367
Uxbridge, MA 01569

Cleckheaton
distributed by
Plymouth Yarns

Coats & Clark
Attn: Consumer Service
P.O. Box 12229
Greenville, SC 29612-0229
www.coatsandclark.com

Debbie Bliss
distributed by
Knitting Fever, Inc.

Filatura Di Crosa
distributed by
Tahki•Stacy Charles, Inc.

Knitting Fever, Inc.
P. O. Box 502
Roosevelt, NY 11575

Lion Brand Yarns
34 West 15th Street
New York, NY 10011
www.lionbrand.com

Patons®
PO Box 40
Listowel, ON N4W 3H3
Canada
www.patonsyarns.com

Plymouth Yarn
PO Box 28
Bristol, PA 19007

Rowan Yarns
4 Townsend West, Unit 8
Nashua, NH 03063

Tahki Yarns
distributed by
Tahki•Stacy Charles, Inc.

Tahki•Stacy Charles, Inc.
8000 Cooper Ave., Bldg. 1
Glendale, NY 11385
Tel: (800) 338-YARN
tahki@worldnet.att.net

TLC
distributed by
Coats & Clark

We have made every effort to ensure the accuracy of the contents of this publication.
We are not responsible for any human or typographical errors.